WINNING WOMEN'S SOFTBALL:
A Complete Guide
for Players and Coaches

Karen Linde and Robert G. Hoehn

PRENTICE HALL
Englewood Cliffs, New Jersey 07632

© 1985 by

PRENTICE-HALL, INC.

Photos by Kathleen Knies

Library of Congress Cataloging in Publication Data

Linde, Karen
  Winning women's softball.

  Includes index.
  1. Softball for women.   2. Softball for women—
Coaching.   I. Hoehn, Robert G.   II. Title.
GV881.L56   1985   796.357'8   85-3653

ISBN 0-13-356734-6
ISBN 0-13-356148-8 PBK

How This Book Will Help You

"What can I do to help my players improve?" *Winning Women's Softball: A Complete Guide for Players and Coaches* answers this question in every chapter by providing timely tips and suggestions for the coach to pass along to each athlete. In this book, you'll find over 150 drills, activities, and games to help you prepare athletes for the coming season. This practical guide works hand in hand with you by:

- Providing challenging, fast-moving activities that help players improve throughout the season.

- Arousing player interest and motivation through competitive games. Gamelike activities appear throughout the book. For example, chapters 7 and 8 stress fielding games that teach sound fundamentals.

- Permitting athletes to work in small groups. Nearly every chapter offers activities and drills for two or more players.

- Listing individual exercises for helping players ready their muscles for action.

- Describing aggressive sliding drills and games for every player (chapter 10).

- Describing game-winning defensive strategy for the entire team (chapter 9).
- Providing small- and large-group hitting drills, activities, and games.
- Providing step-by-step preseason, in-season, and post-season conditioning activities (chapter 13).
- Including chapters on how athletes can improve their fielding, throwing, and baserunning skills.
- Providing tips in nearly every chapter for the coach on how to help athletes play their positions or refine their playing skills.

Photographs, charts, and illustrations have been carefully selected to help you prepare for a winning season.

Karen Linde

Robert G. Hoehn

Contents

8: *Outfield* *93*

Preparing the Outfielder for Competition *(93)* Warm-Up Exercises for Outfielders *(94)* Teaching the Proper Throwing Grip *(95)* Showing Outfielders How to Make Accurate Throws *(96)* Four Fast-Moving Partner Throwing Drills *(99)* Group Competitive Throwing Drills *(100)* Fielding Grounders, Line Drives, and Fly Balls *(104)* Fielding Games for Two, Three, and Four Players *(107)* Tips and Suggestions for Playing the Outfield *(111)* Points to Remember *(113)*

9: *Defensive Team Play* *115*

Guidelines for Setting Up Practice Sessions *(115)* Cut-Off and Relay Patterns *(116)* Pop-Up Assignments *(125)* Wild Pitch Assignments *(126)* Bunt Plays *(126)* Rundown Plays *(128)* Fast-Action Defensive Drills *(130)* Points to Remember *(132)*

10: *The Running Game* *133*

Developing a Successful Running Game *(133)* Setting Up Running Situations *(134)* Baserunning Drills *(138)* Examining Three Sliding Techniques *(140)* Fast-Action Sliding Drills *(143)* Tips and Suggestions for Baserunning and Sliding *(146)* Points to Remember *(146)*

11: *Bunting* *149*

The Sacrifice Bunt *(149)* Two-, Three-, and Four-Player Bunting Drills *(152)* Bunting for the Base Hit *(158)* Base-Hit Bunting Drills *(158)* Building Confidence in Bunting *(161)* Tips and Suggestions for Better Bunting *(162)* Points to Remember *(162)*

12: *Hitting* *163*

Examining the Physical Side of Hitting *(163)* Examining the Mental Side of Hitting *(166)* Individual Hitting Drills and Activities *(167)* Small-Group Hitting Drills, Activities, and Games *(169)* Hitting Drills for the Entire Team *(174)* Ways to Help Athletes Break the Batting Slump *(178)* Tips and Suggestions for Successful Hitting *(182)* Points to Remember *(183)*

13: *Activities for the Off-Season* *185*

What Should Your Players Do in the Off-Season? *(185)* What Should You Do During the Off-Season? *(186)* Conditioning Programs and Activities *(188)* How Your Athletes Can Ready Themselves for the Coming Season *(189)* Points to Remember *(190)*

Index *191*

1. Pitching

IT HAS BEEN SAID that pitching is anywhere from 70 to 90 percent of the game. So much depends on the pitcher's ability to throw strikes consistently and keep the batter off balance.

This chapter examines the following areas:

1. Preparing pitchers to take the mound
2. Two-pitcher conditioning drills
3. Examining the mechanics of pitching
4. Developing the four basic pitches
5. Drills for improving accuracy
6. Effective communication between pitchers and catchers
7. Three-pitcher fielding drills
8. Ways to keep pitchers mentally alert
9. Setting up an early season practice plan for pitchers
10. Points to remember

Let's begin with a series of loosening exercises and related activities.

PREPARING PITCHERS TO TAKE THE MOUND

As a coach, you select a conditioning program that fits your practice schedule and complements your coaching style. The trick is to find and develop activities that will help pitchers reach their optimum level of performance in a reasonable length of time. This takes intelligent planning, fresh energy, and common sense. You must be careful not to overwork your pitchers and, at the same time, prepare them adequately for competition.

Some coaches make the mistake of thinking all pitchers stick to a workout schedule, especially a pre- or off-season training program. They don't. A wise coach will begin practice at a slow but steady pace. Then as pitchers begin to get into shape the coach will increase conditioning activities to keep pace with development.

A pitcher should warm up before beginning practice. Here are seven warm-up exercises that a pitcher can do on her own:

1. Stand erect with feet shoulder width apart. Place hands on hips. Turn hips to the left at far as possible. Point right elbow at left foot. Hold position for five seconds. Return to original position. Now turn hips to the right as far as possible. Point left elbow at right foot. Repeat procedure five times.

2. Stand erect with feet shoulder width apart. Raise arms sideward to slightly above shoulder height, palms upward. Slowly pull arms back as far as possible. Relax the arms momentarily and then repeat the pull. Repeat procedure 20 times.

3. Stand erect with feet shoulder width apart. Stretch out by extending arm high above head, arching back, and lifting body weight by standing on toes. Hold position for ten seconds. Repeat procedure five or six times.

4. Sit on ground with legs spread shoulder width apart. Bend forward, keep knees straight, and grab the soles of the feet. Try to touch the ground with head. Hold position for 20 seconds. Repeat procedure three or four times.

5. Rest on stomach, arch back, and grab ankles from behind. Hyperextend head and neck as much as possible. Hold position for 20 seconds. Repeat procedure three or four times.

6. Stand erect with arms along side of body. Begin swinging pitching arm back and forth in pendulum fashion. After five swings bring arm around in a complete circle simulating the pitching motion. Make five full circles, increasing speed with each circle.

7. Hang from an overhead bar with both hands. Don't let feet touch the ground. Let arm support body weight. Now release the non-throwing hand from the bar. Hold body weight for five seconds. Repeat procedure five times.

Have pitchers loosen their arms by playing easy toss, that is, by finding a partner (preferably pitcher or catcher) and making easy overhand throws for approximately ten minutes. Encourage them to concentrate on following through completely with each toss.

When an athlete's arm begins to warm, the creative juices start to flow and thoughts may turn to horseplay. A pitcher (or any player) may punish her arm by throwing overhead curve balls, sidearm "freak" pitches, or anything else famous for developing sore arms. You can reduce horseplay by introducing two simple throwing games designed to stress basic fundamentals. They work like this:

Game One

Partners stand about 50 feet apart. Player 1, tosser, bounces a ground ball to Player 2, fielder. Player 2 fields the ball and throws it to Player 1. If the ball (according to Player 1) enters the strike zone, Player 2 receives one point. After fielding and throwing four balls, Player 2 becomes tosser and Player 1 becomes fielder. The athlete who earns the most points in five minutes wins the game.

Game Two

The procedure is the same as "Game One" with one exception: The tosser delivers high fly balls to the fielder.

A good way for pitchers to finish warming their arms is to have them make several (eight to ten) long throws. For instance, two throws at 55 feet, two throws at 60 feet, and so on. Pitchers stay busy for 20 minutes while concentrating on basic fundamentals and engaging in friendly competition.

TWO-PITCHER CONDITIONING DRILLS

Most coaches give their pitchers extra running drills, both long distance and sprints. In fact, with few exceptions, pitchers run more than anyone else on the team. Since a pitcher's endurance and stamina come from her legs, she must work hard to get them in shape. The following five conditioning drills serve to strengthen a pitcher's legs while she fields and throws the ball.

Step-back Pickups

Partners, wearing gloves, face each other and stand about 20 or 25 feet apart. Partner 1, tosser, begins the drill by rolling a ball to the right or left of Partner 2, fielder. Partner 2 fields the ball with two hands and makes an overhand throw to Partner 1. After fielding four balls, Partner 1 calls out "step back." Partner 2 takes two steps backward. Play continues until both players are about 35 feet apart. Each time Player 1 shouts "step back," she should make wider tosses to Player 2. After 10 or 12 tosses, Partners switch positions and continue play.

Lateral/Toss

Partners bring their gloves and a ball to an open area. They stand about 90 feet away and face each other. Action starts when Player 1, runner, holds a ball and runs at full speed toward Player 2, tosser. When she gets within ten feet of Player 2, Player 1 tosses her the ball and continues to run straight ahead. Player 2 hollers, "Break Left" or "Break Right," and throws the ball in the called direction. Player 1 fields the ball and continues play by running the same pattern again. Only this time Player 1 starts running toward Player 2 from where she fielded the ball.

Players switch positions after five or six tosses: runner becomes tosser, tosser becomes runner. Each athlete should field at least ten balls.

Dead Ball/Live Ball

Partners bring their gloves and a ball to an open area. They stand about 50 feet away and face each other. Player 1, tosser, places a ball about 40 feet to the right of Player 2, fielder. Action begins when Player 1 yells "Go." Player 2 breaks to her right, picks up the ball, throws it to Player 1. She then sprints full speed to her original starting position. Player 1 tosses a line drive, bouncing ball, or high fly to Player 2. Player 2 fields and throws to Player 1. Player 2 returns to her starting position. Player 1 places the ball about 40 feet to the left of Player 2 and action continues. Partners switch positions after four tosses.

Fetch

Partners bring their gloves and a ball to an open area. They stand next to each other about six feet apart. Action begins when Player 1, tosser, yells, "Go." Player 2, fielder, runs straight ahead at full speed. Player 1 counts off four seconds and hollers, "Catch," and throws the ball to Player 2. The tosser should throw a deep ball or one that forces the fielder to extend her arm and body to make a catch. After Player 2 fields the ball, she throws it back to Player 1 and returns to her original position. Player 2 fields three balls before changing positions with Player 1.

Right Sprint/Left Sprint

Partners bring their gloves and a ball to an open area. They stand next to each other, about six feet apart. Action begins when Player 1, tosser, yells, "Go." Player 2, fielder, runs straight ahead at full speed. Player 1 shouts "Right," Player 2 breaks to her right and fields a thrown ball. As soon as she fields the ball and makes a return throw, Player 1 yells "Left" and tosses a high, lofting ball to Player 2. Player 2 fields four balls before changing positions with Player 1.

EXAMINING THE MECHANICS OF PITCHING

The windmill motion is the preferred style of pitching. Therefore, in this section we'll stress the mechanics of developing the windmill pitcher.

Here's an example of a checklist you can use to monitor the progress of your pitchers (right-handers) during practice:

Stance	*Coach's Comment*
1. Takes a comfortable stance, feet approximately shoulder width apart.	1.
2. Hooks ball of right foot over the front of the rubber (Figure 1.1.).	2.
3. Touches the back part of the rubber with the toe of the left foot.	3.
4. Uses a firm, but loose grip.	4.

Delivery	
1. Leans slightly backward, then shifts weight forward as pitching motion begins (Figure 1.2).	1.
2. Bends forward at the waist as arm is brought up; locks wrist (Figure 1.3).	2.
3. Fully extends arm above head; turns left hip toward third base	3.
4. Moves hips and shoulders in unison.	4.
5. Touches left heel to ground; points toes upward (Figure 1.4).	5.
6. Points left foot straight forward toward target (Figure 1.5).	6.

7. Keeps the length of the step consistent. 7.

8. Pushes the right foot hard off rubber. 8.

Release

1. Uncocks wrist and snaps wrist quickly 1.
   as ball is released (Figure 1.6).

2. Keeps the head still. 2.

3. Keeps body in an upright position. 3.

Figure 1.1

Figure 1.2

Figure 1.3

Figure 1.4

Figure 1.5

Figure 1.6

Follow-through

1. Follows through with arm. Both wrist   1.
   and hips snap simultaneously.

2. Lands on the heel first, then the toe.   2.

3. Keeps knees slightly bent.   3.

4. Finishes with the feet approximately   4.
   shoulder width apart, square to the
   catcher, ready to field (Figure 1.7).

Figure 1.7

Some coaches believe that the key to developing a topnotch wind-mill pitcher lies in the whip action of her delivery. The following plan helps a pitcher develop a strong, whiplike motion and quick release:

Equipment: Balls, gloves, and a movable rubber plate.

Procedure: Pitchers find a partner (preferably a catcher) and stand about 15 feet apart. Pitchers can work alone by tossing a "softie" ball against a wall.

Step 1:

- Pitcher stands with left shoulder and left hip facing home plate. Place feet at about a 45-degree angle to home plate (Figure 1.8).

- Cock wrist. Swing arm back to shoulder level. Then bring arm forward in pitching motion keeping arm as close to body as possible. *Whip arm through*, uncock wrist, and release ball in the hip area.

- *Do not move the feet.* Note: The forearm may hit the hip when whipping through. This will occur at first, but it isn't necessary to hit the hip with any amount of force to be an effective pitcher.

Figure 1.8

Step 2:

- Repeat procedure. This time *take one step forward with left foot*, keeping toes pointed at the target or anywhere between home plate and a 45-degree angle (Figure 1.9).

- Place body weight on right foot while bringing the right arm back.

- On the down whip, step forward on the left foot. Then shift the body weight to left foot as the arm whips through. At this point the hips should face the target and the right heel should be off the ground.

Step 3:

- Repeat procedure. Now *swing the arm back over the head before whipping it through.*

- As the arm swings back and passes the midline of the body, the upper arm should brush against the hair and the wrist should rotate so that the ball faces the third base side.

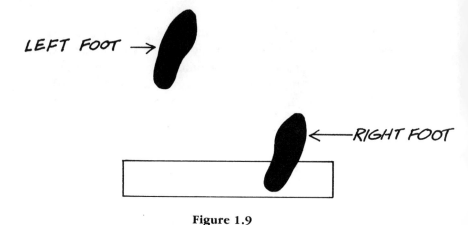

Figure 1.9

Step 4:

• Repeat Step 3, with one exception: Use the step and weight shift as described in Step 2.

Step 5:

• Same as Step 1, except use a *full* windmill motion.
• Hold ball in both hands in front of body. Bring right arm straight up. The back of the hand should be up as the arm reaches the head. The upper arm should rub against the hair. When the ball reaches the top of the arch, the wrist should rotate so that the ball faces third base. At this point the arm whips through the downswing bringing the arm as close to the hip as possible.

Once a pitcher develops a smooth delivery and gains confidence, you can help her increase velocity by having her stress these six points:

• Concentrate on a quick release with a fast wrist snap.
• Use a full arm extension at the top of the windmill.
• Slightly bend the elbow of the pitching arm prior to windup. Then windup with a fast arm spin.
• Turn hip in conjunction with the release.

- Bend left knee on the follow-through.
- Follow through completely after releasing the ball.

You can use the checklist to pinpoint, isolate, and correct problems as pitchers work off the mound.

DEVELOPING THE FOUR BASIC PITCHES

How many different pitches a hurler throws depends on such factors as physical ability, opponent's hitting strength, game situation, and coaching philosophy.

A pitcher runs the risk of losing her composure if she tries to master too many pitches. Many coaches like their pitchers to throw four basic pitches—fastball, change-up, rise, and drop. Coaches agree that throwing strikes and changing speeds are a pitcher's bread and butter.

Here are tips and suggestions for teaching your pitchers how to throw the four basic pitches:

1. Fastball

Grip

- Grip ball across the seams, fingers spread comfortably apart (Figure 1.10). Press the fleshy part of the upper fingers against the seams. Use the thumb and little finger to help balance the ball.
- Use a firm, but relaxed grip. Hold the ball in the upper part of the hand.

Windup

- Hold head still, fix eyes on target.
- Cock the wrist and relax elbow throughout delivery.
- Use a full arm extension, high over head.
- Push hard off the mound, relax lead leg, and whip arm around.

Release

- Employ whip action off the hip prior to release.
- Release the ball at the same point each time.
- Rotate the hips and trunk in unison.
- Uncock wrist as hand reaches hip area. Whip the ball forward with a quick wrist snap.

Figure 1.10

Follow-through

- Follow through completely on every pitch.
- Keep the stride length the same with each pitch.
- Finish with feet squarely facing home plate, body weight shifted over balls of feet, glove held waist high in front of body.

2. Change-up

Grip

- Hold ball firmly and deeply in the palm of the hand (Figure 1.11). The windup, release, and follow-through are the same as the fastball.

3. Rise

Grip

- Hold ball across seams for maximum four-seam rotational spin (Figure 1.12). Keep the index and middle finger together. Note: The number of fingers on the ball varies with pitchers. Some prefer to place three fingers in the middle and separate them (Figure 1.13); others tuck the index finger up on the seams (Figure 1.14).

Figure 1.11

Figure 1.12

Figure 1.13

Figure 1.14

13

The windup, release, and follow-through are essentially the same as the fastball with these exceptions:

Windup

- Keep arm and wrist close to body.
- Dip down with shoulders slightly and hold head low. Keep head and shoulders forward.

Release

- Snap wrist, arm, and forearm upward to create a rapid spin on the ball.
- Roll ball over the inside of the middle finger and the first joint of the index finger.
- Bring hand under the ball at point of release.
- Keep wrist, forearm, and hand in a straight line as they pass the hips. Keep shoulders back to accentuate the back spin.

Follow-through

- Continue to turn the wrist and throw hand in front of face.

Have pitchers practice their fast upward snap release by following this procedure: Find a partner. Bring gloves and a ball to an open area. Stand about 20 feet apart and face each other. Player 2, pitcher, holds the ball outward directly behind her, even with the hip. She steps forward and fires it to Player 2, catcher. Player 2 gives a waist-high target and carefully observes the pitcher as she releases and follows through. After the delivery the catcher makes corrections as needed. After ten pitches athletes switch positions and continue play. *Note:* Stress that pitchers concentrate on releasing the ball with a strong forward and upward wrist snap.

If the ball doesn't rise, have the catcher check these points:

- Hand position upon release. Should be under ball.
- Wrist snap upon release. Should be forceful.
- Cocked wrist. May be uncocking wrist too soon.
- Stride length. May be too short.
- Hand position after release. Should be in front of face.

4. Drop

Grip

- Hold the ball across the seams for maximum speed (lifting action). Place thumb in front of ball with fingers resting behind (Figure 1.15).
- Hold the ball along the seams (rolling action). Place thumb underneath ball with fingers coming over (Figure 1.16).

Figure 1.15

Figure 1.16

Windup

- Keep head and shoulders leaning slightly forward.
- Thrust hips and shoulders upward to create a greater spin.
- Keep back of hand pointing toward third base.

Release

- Turn arm and hand over and snap wrist down. Throw hand and forearm over and down across left knee (right-hander).

Follow-through

- Push hard off the pitcher's mound.
- Follow through completely.

You might want to show your pitchers another way to throw a drop. It works like this:

Have them grip the ball with two or three fingers across the seams balancing it with the thumb and little finger (Figure 1.17). Prior to releasing the ball, tell them to pull their fingers hard and fast in an upward direction against the seams. This will create a spin allowing the ball to drop with little or no curve.

Figure 1.17

Have pitchers practice throwing the drop with a partner as they did the rise ball. If the ball doesn't drop, have the catcher check these points:

- Slow release. May not be turning hand and forearm over and down hard enough or pulling fingers up against seams hard enough.
- May be releasing the ball too late.
- Striding too far off the mound.

A young pitcher needs plenty of time to develop her repertoire of pitches. Practice, persistence, and patience are the keys for molding a tough competitor. Once a pitcher consistently throws strikes across home plate, she's ready to sharpen her control and go for the corners.

DRILLS FOR IMPROVING ACCURACY

A smart pitcher doesn't try to increase control by reducing the speed of the pitch or by aiming the ball. She concentrates on varying her pitches, setting up the hitter, and throwing the ball where the batter is least likely to make solid contact. Naturally this requires hours of hard practice, intense concentration, and a strong desire to succeed.

The following drills will help pitchers concentrate on throwing strikes. These drills require a pitcher and catcher (or two pitchers), softballs, gloves, and a movable rubber plate, if necessary.

Three and Two

An imaginary batter has a count of three balls and two strikes. The catcher signals and sets her target. The pitcher must hit the target or she loses the batter. The catcher acts as umpire. Each time a batter walks a run is scored against the pitcher. The idea, of course, is to throw a strike *every* time. If two pitchers participate, have them trade off pitching and catching. The player with the fewest runs charged against her wins.

You can liven up the drills by including any of these situations:

- Number of pitches—10; last inning—pitcher's team is ahead three to zero.
- Number of pitches—8; last inning—pitcher's team is ahead three to one.
- Number of pitches—6; top of the sixth inning—no score. Partners trade off pitching and catching until game ends.

Tire Target

Tie an old tire against the backstop or sideline fence. The pitcher earns one point for each ball that passes through the open space in the center of the tire. The partner acts as judge and retrieves the balls. After ten pitches athletes switch positions. The game ends when each athlete throws 30 pitches. The player with the most points wins.

Carpet Target

Tie a carpet square (represents the strike zone) against the backstop or sideline fence. Paint a six-inch circle or square in each corner of the carpet, and one in the center. Each player receives ten pitches to hit one of the painted targets. If a pitch hits a corner target, the pitcher earns three points. If a pitch strikes the center target, the hurler earns one point. The partner acts as judge and retrieves the balls. After ten pitches athletes switch positions. The game ends when each athlete throws 30 pitches. The player with the most points wins.

Beat Your Partner

Bring two movable rubber plates to an open area. Partners take turns pitching half-innings (three outs) to one another.

The drill begins when the catcher gives a target and calls the pitch; i.e., rise, high inside corner or fastball, low inside corner, and so on. The catcher records balls and strikes. A strikeout equals an out; a walk means a run. The pitcher and catcher switch roles after *each* pitch; that is, they take turns pitching to one another. The player who walks the fewest batters in three innings wins.

EFFECTIVE COMMUNICATION
BETWEEN PITCHERS AND CATCHERS

A pitcher gains valuable experience when she coordinates her efforts with the catcher. The catcher, in many instances, determines how effective the pitcher will be. A smart catcher can help a floundering pitcher by spotting flaws in her pitching motion, calling pitches that batters have trouble hitting solidly, and shouting continual words of encouragement.

The following pitcher/catcher drills are excellent for developing pitcher control and self-confidence.

Catcher's-Glove Drill

This drill can be conducted anywhere on the softball diamond or sideline areas of the playing field. A good way to begin is by having two pitchers take turns throwing the ball to the catcher. In this way each pitcher can take a short rest between pitches.

The drill begins when the catcher takes a crouching stance behind home plate (movable rubber base). The pitcher delivers the ball to the catcher's glove. The drill stays alive by the catcher moving her target to various spots around home plate. The pitcher concentrates on hitting five specific areas of home plate; high and low inside corners, high and low outside corners, and directly over the center of home plate. Once the pitcher repeatedly hits her target, she then changes her style of pitches (fast ball, change-up, drop, etc.) and continues the same pattern of throwing.

Stringed-Target Drill

Little equipment is needed to construct the apparatus for this drill. Use two rounded wooden poles approximately six feet long and an inch and a half wide. The rounded poles prevent the pitched ball from becoming scraped. Mark off the strike zone with chalk line. Place the poles firmly in the ground (Figure 1.18).

The catcher, wearing a mask, takes her normal stance behind home plate. The pitcher concentrates on throwing the ball inside the marked target areas. Again, when the pitcher consistently throws strikes, she alternates pitches—change-up, drop, rise, and fastball.

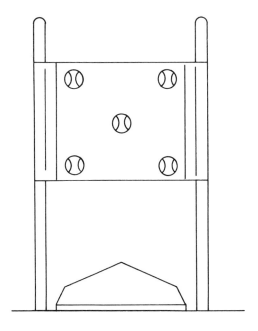

Figure 1.18

Batter-Weakness Drill

The object is for the pitcher to throw the ball to the area around home plate where the batter has a difficult time making solid contact with the ball. Both catcher and pitcher must study each hitter's stance, grip, stride, and swing in order to determine particular weaknesses.

The batting cage or backstop offers a satisfactory place to perform this drill.

The coach or a designated player may act as hitter. Her job is to stand at home plate holding a bat while assuming a variety of batting styles using different strides, stances, and grips. She should make no attempt to swing at the ball. As the hitter demonstrates different batting styles, the catcher watches for apparent weaknesses and moves her target accordingly. The pitcher concentrates on hitting each target given by the catcher.

The chart below lists the pitches thrown to different batting styles.

Batting Style	Pitches
Overstriding	High and inside fastball; change-up
Short stride	Low and inside fast pitch
Little or no choke on bat	High or low inside fast pitch
High choke on bat	High or low outside fast pitch
Tight grip on bat	High or low inside fast pitch
Stepping "in the bucket"	High or low outside fast pitch
Crowds the plate	High or low inside fast pitch
Upper cutter	Pitch high
Squares to bunt	Inside and outside fast pitch
Drops shoulder when swinging	High fast pitch

The key to a pitcher's strength is in recognizing individual batting weaknesses and working with her catcher in pitching to these weak spots. A pitcher can keep the hitters off balance by varying her pitches while throwing to these areas.

Effective communication between pitchers and catchers should include the following:

- Finding out what pitches are working.
- An evaluation of overall pitching performance; i.e., is the pitcher using a variety of pitches? Is the pitcher hurrying her throws or

aiming the ball? Is the pitcher staying ahead of the batters? Is the pitcher aware of game conditions; i.e., position of teammates, weather conditions, etc.? Is the pitcher maintaining self-control?

- A clear understanding of signals and strategy to be employed at different times.

THREE-PITCHER FIELDING DRILLS

A good fielding pitcher is a plus for the defense. She is not afraid to move about, field bunts, and back up throws from the outfielders. Her aggressive play makes her a true competitor.

Here are five basic fielding drills for pitchers working in groups of three. (*Note:* Two pitchers and a catcher may work together.)

Follow-through

Purpose: To follow through completely and be ready to field the ball.

Three athletes bring their gloves, a movable rubber base, and a ball to an open area. Player 1, pitcher, and Player 2, catcher, take their positions. Player 3, fielder, stands about 50 feet directly behind Player 1. The movable rubber base acts as home plate.

Action begins when Player 1 winds up and throws to Player 2. After releasing the ball Player 1 finishes her pitch with both feet parallel to each other, ready to move in any direction. She holds her glove about waist-high in front of her body. Player 2 fires the ball back at the pitcher—either a one hopper, line drive, or low-bouncing grounder. A fast shot back up the middle convinces the pitcher to set quickly and be ready to knock anything down. Player 3 acts as backup for balls that get past the pitcher.

Athletes switch positions after six chances. Player 1 becomes Player 2, Player 2 becomes Player 3, and so on.

Get 'Em at Second

Purpose: To make accurate throws to second base.

Three athletes bring their gloves, two movable rubber bases, and a ball to an open area. Player 1, pitcher, and Player 2, catcher, take their positions. Player 3, fielder, places a rubber base at second. The idea is to get a force-out at second base.

Action begins when Player 1 delivers a pitch to Player 2. After catching the ball Player 2 tosses a grounder back at the pitcher or near a baseline and shouts "Second." Pitcher fields the ball, turns, and makes a chest-high, glove-side throw to Player 3. Player 3 breaks for second when the catcher tosses the ball on the ground. *Note:* A "hurry up" throw to second often winds up in center field. The pitcher must field the ball cleanly before attempting to throw.

Athletes switch positions after six chances as they did in Drill One.

Break Left

Purpose: To practice getting a fast jump toward first base.

Three athletes bring their gloves, a movable rubber base, and a ball to an open area. Player 1, pitcher, and Player 2, catcher, take their positions. Player 3, fielder, places a rubber base at first.

Action begins when Player 1 delivers a pitch to Player 2. After catching the ball, Player 2 tosses a grounder to the right of Player 3. Player 1 breaks quickly to her left and sprints toward first base. Player 3 fields and throws to Player 1 covering first base. *Note:* This play requires the pitcher to break quickly to her left whenever a batter hits the ball between first and second base. The pitcher should take the throw while running parallel to the baseline. Athletes switch positions after six chances as they did in Drill One.

Slow Bouncer

Purpose: To get an out on a slow-bouncing ground ball.

Three athletes bring their gloves, a movable rubber base, and a ball to an open area. Player 1, pitcher, and Player 2, catcher, take their positions. Player 3, fielder, places a rubber base at first.

Action begins when Player 1 delivers a pitch to Player 2. After catching the ball Player 2 tosses a slow-bouncing ball toward the pitcher or down a baseline. (Situation: Runner on First). Player 1 charges the ball, hears Player 2 yell "First," and throws to Player 3 covering first base. *Note:* The catcher has the play in front of her and can advise the pitcher on where to throw the ball. Few runners are thrown out at second on a slow-bouncing ball unless they trip or simply lack speed afoot. Athletes switch positions after six chances as they did in Drill One.

First, Second, Third

Purpose: To field bunted balls and make accurate throws
to the baseman.

Three athletes bring their gloves, a movable rubber base, and a ball to an open area. Player 1, pitcher, and Player 2, catcher, take their positions. Player 3, fielder, acts as the first, second, and third baseman and uses the rubber base accordingly. She starts out the drill at first base.

Action begins when Player 1 delivers a pitch to Player 2. After catching the ball Player 2 flips a slow, buntlike ball onto the infield and yells "First." The pitcher charges, fields, and makes a throw to first. Player 1 fields three balls before Player 3 picks up the base, moves to second, and becomes a second baseman.

Play continues as before with the catcher shouting "Second." The pitcher fields and throws three times to second base. Finally Player 3 goes to third, catcher hollers "Third," and the pitcher fields and throws three more times.

After nine chances athletes switch positions as they did in Drill One. *Note:* On bunt situations the pitcher must fire off the mound quickly, listen for directions from the catcher, and make an accurate chest-high, glove-side throw to the baseman.

WAYS TO KEEP PITCHERS MENTALLY ALERT

A pitcher may lose concentration because of a distraction or nervousness or lack of confidence or anything else that serves to throw off her timing. Again, a wise catcher who keeps her head in the game can help a pitcher stay in command. A pitcher, however, must prepare herself mentally before entering competition.

Here are guidelines to give pitchers for developing the mental side of pitching:

1. Know what you can and can't do. Keep a positive outlook at all times.

2. Keep an open mind. As an individual, you will develop your own style and method of pitching, but be willing to try new ideas and methods.

3. Set realistic goals. Know what you want and how you plan on getting there. Break each goal into simple measurable units. For instance, one goal might be to walk no more than one batter per game or strike out at least one batter per inning or maintain poise on the mound during rough moments.

A plan to help you reach each goal is as follows:

- After analyzing what skills or abilities are necessary to reach each goal, set your mind to expect success as you participate in practice sessions and games.

- Think positive and visualize success. Visualization works well during game situations. When you are on the mound, for example, picture the pitch you will deliver and where it is going to go or end up.

Never worry about the batter except to make sure the ball goes where you know it will do the most good. Pitch to the target, not the batter.

When you are alone you can mentally rehearse through simulation by fixing in your mind's eye the strike zone. Before actually "releasing" the ball you: (1) take your position on the pitcher's mound; (2) receive the signal from the catcher; (3) study the catcher's target—i.e., low inside corner; (4) present the ball to the batter; (5) grip the ball for the type of pitch you will deliver; (6) deliver the ball to the batter; (7) hit the target dead center.

Now see yourself moving the ball around home plate chipping away at the edges (Figure 1.19). The idea is to pick a number in the strike zone and mentally toss strikes. If this seems silly, then here's something to remember: Visualization is a technique based on the ability of the autonomic nervous system to translate mental images into physical action.

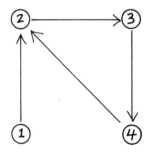

Figure 1.19

**SETTING UP AN EARLY SEASON PRACTICE PLAN
FOR PITCHERS**

A well-organized, two-hour practice session should keep pitchers busy with challenging activities. The secret is to sustain player interest by changing activities often and stressing those skills necessary for success.

Here is a sample schedule showing how the drills, games, and activities outlined in this section can help prepare pitchers for action.

Day	5 Min.	10 Min.	15–20 Min.	20 Min.	20 Min.	20 Min.	20 Min.
M	Jog	Easy Toss	Warm-up Game #1; Long Toss	Coaching Checklist: Developing Whip Action Delivery	Control Drill: Catcher's Glove Drill	Dead Ball/ Live Ball; Fetch	Stepback Pickups; Wind Sprints
T	Jog	Easy Toss	Warm-up Game #2; Long Toss	Coaching Checklist: Developing Whip Action Delivery	Fielding Drill: Follow-Through	Lateral/ Toss; Right Sprint, Left Sprint	Stepback Pickups; Wind Sprints
W	Jog	Easy Toss	Warm-up Game #1; Long Toss	Coaching Checklist: Developing Increased Velocity	Control Drill: Stringed Target Drill	Get 'Em at Second; Break Left	Dead Ball/ Live Ball; Wind Sprints
Th	Jog	Easy Toss	Warm-up Game #2; Long Toss	Coaching Checklist: Developing Increased Velocity	Fielding Drill: First, Second, Third	Lateral/ Toss; Fetch	Right Sprint/ Left Sprint; Wind Sprints
F	Jog	Easy Toss	Warm-up Game #1; Long Toss	Coaching Checklist: Developing Increased Velocity	Accuracy Drill: Beat Your Partner	Slow Bouncer; Follow Through	Stepback Pickups; Wind Sprints

An early season practice plan should include:

1. Lively activities ranging from 10 to 20 minutes in length. If activities drag on, athletes become bored, lose interest, and waste time.
2. Plenty of stretching exercises and running.
3. Drills that emphasize fielding and throwing.
4. Activities that are challenging and fun.
5. Activities that allow the coach or teammate to pinpoint problem areas and lend assistance.
6. Alternate activities to compensate for inclement weather or emergency situations.
7. Activities that keep pace with the athlete's progress.
8. Activities commensurate with coaching philosophy, coaching style, and overall goals of the program.

POINTS TO REMEMBER

Good pitching can make an ordinary team look outstanding.

A smart pitcher readies herself, both mentally and physically. As she goes, so goes the team.

There is no substitute for hard practice. This season's young, inexperienced pitcher is next year's veteran. So much depends on attitude and the desire to be the very best.

The pitcher should believe in herself and her ability to succeed. If she does, the good days will outnumber the rough ones.

2. Catching

CATCHING IS PERHAPS the toughest position on the field to play. It takes an athlete with a "take charge" personality, a good throwing arm, and the ability to handle pitchers in a positive manner.

We'll review the following areas in this section:

1. Preparing catchers for action
2. Examining the mechanics of catching
3. Individual drills for catchers
4. Small group drills for catchers
5. Tips and suggestions for the catcher
6. Points to remember

PREPARING CATCHERS FOR ACTION

Catching requires an athlete to give her body, especially her legs, a hard workout by constantly shifting from side to side, moving up and down, and crouching in a squat position. To be successful, a catcher must have strong legs, good speed, and the ability to make quick moves.

Here are five early season conditioning exercises you can give catchers to strengthen their legs:

1. Assume a crouching stance. Spread feet shoulder width apart and shift body weight slightly over balls of feet. Fold arms. Now

come to a standing position by slowly pushing off the toes. Hold position for five seconds. Return to crouching stance. Repeat ten times.

2. Assume kneeling position. Sit back on heels. Extend arms over head and lean back. Reach back as far as possible. Hold for five seconds. Repeat ten times.

3. Assume duck walk position. Keep hands behind back. Duck walk approximately 30 feet, turn around, and return to starting position. Repeat five times.

4. Assume a crouching stance about 30 feet away and facing a wall. Toss a rubber ball or tennis ball against the wall. Field the rebound and repeat the procedure at least 30 times.

5. Bring glove and softball to an open area. Assume a crouching stance. Toss ball to the left. After it stops rolling, fire out of the chute, scoop up the ball, simulate a throw to first base, and return to original position. Repeat procedure nine times. Alternate simulating throws to each base and rolling balls to the left and right.

EXAMINING THE MECHANICS OF CATCHING

In this section we'll look at the catcher's ability to throw, block, and field. We'll study seven different catching techniques, how she can practice them, and how she can correct any problems that occur.

Have your catcher(s) concentrate on these points:

Stance

Regular Crouching Position

- Crouch behind home plate, right foot slightly forward of left foot.
- Stay up on toes with weight evenly balanced over feet. Spread feet comfortably apart.
- Rest right hand against inside of right thigh. Use glove and right leg to hide signals from opposing base coaches (Figure 2.1).
- Stay directly behind home plate, face the pitcher, and leave enough room between you and the batter to prevent interfering with her swing.
- Give signal to the pitcher. Then tuck thumb of bare hand under fingers and make a fist. This will minimize injuries to the fingers and thumb from foul tips.
- Give pitcher a clear target.

Figure 2.1

Receiving Position

- Lean forward and raise up slightly. Hold arms, flexed at elbows, out in front. Keep weight evenly distributed over balls of feet.
- Point the pocket of the mitt at the pitcher.
- Keep the barehand fist clinched until you catch the ball. Then open fist and cup hand over the ball.
- If the pitch is above your waist, hold glove with fingers pointing upward; if the pitch is below your waist, hold glove with fingers pointing downward.

Shifting Feet

- On inside pitches, move the right foot to the left and step to the side with the left foot. This soon becomes a quick, sliding motion when repeated several times.
- On outside pitches, move the left foot to the right and step to the side with the right foot.

You can have your catcher practice shifting her feet in the following manner: Go to the mound or an open area. Stand about 40 feet away and face the catcher. Have her take a crouching stance. Then simulate the pitching motion, including the follow-through. After releasing the "ball," holler "inside or outside." Check your catcher as she shifts her feet back and forth.

Watch for these common errors:

- Body weight centered over heels.
- Leaning toward first or third while in crouching stance.
- Exposing thumb and fingers to injury.
- Rear end too high off the ground (makes catching the ball more difficult).
- Arms held too close to the body, thus restricting side movement.

The best way to help catchers improve is to correct mistakes the moment they happen. Either model the correct procedure yourself or have the athlete take several trial runs, step by step, until she has a clear understanding of the problem.

Blocking Balls in the Dirt

Ball Bounces in Front of Catcher

- Drop to both knees. Hold mitt between the legs, tipping it slightly forward.
- Keep body in front of the ball (Figure 2.2).

Ball in the Dirt to Catcher's Right

- Step out with right leg and drop to left knee.
- Hold mitt between the legs, tipping it slightly forward.
- Keep body in front of the ball (Figure 2.3).

Ask your catcher, wearing shin guards, to bring her mitt and follow you to the backstop or sideline fence area. Have her assume a crouching position. Stand about 40 feet away and toss balls to her left, right, and directly in front of her.

Watch for these common errors:

- Upper body not tilted forward.
- Catcher attempts to catch rather than block the ball.
- Brings hands up, lifts body, and creates an opening for the ball to go through (on balls bouncing in front of catcher).
- Neglects to keep body in front of the ball.

Figure 2.2

Figure 2.3

Throwing

Grip

- Hold the ball with a cross-seam grip to create a four-seam rotational spin.

Catching and Releasing the Ball

- After catching the ball (right-handed catcher), take a short step with the right foot, and swing left foot around to throw.
- Line the shoulders up for the throw.
- Bring arm back to a point to the rear and side of the right ear.

- Push hard off the right leg and step with the left leg toward the target.
- Release ball with a strong overhand throw.

Here are two target-throwing games that challenge the throwing ability of the catcher.

Percentage Throw

Catcher and two players bring their gloves, a movable rubber base (second base), and a softball to an open area.

Player 1, fielder, acts as a second baseman and holds her glove about two feet above the base. Player 2, back up, stands about 20 feet behind Player 1 and retrieves wild or mishandled throws.

Action begins when the catcher, holding a ball, takes a crouching stance. When Player 2 yells "Go," the catcher makes an overhand throw to second. Player 2 makes no attempt to catch the ball unless the throw is close enough to tag out a runner.

The catcher receives two points for each accurate throw. She makes ten throws. Her score is calculated on a percentage basis. For example, if she earns eight points, her score is 40 percent (8 out of 20). In this drill the catcher can compete against herself or against another catcher.

Glove on a Stick

Catcher and another player bring their gloves (plus an extra glove for the target), a rounded stick (two to three feet long), and a softball to an open area.

Player 1, fielder, stands about 85 feet away from the catcher. She pushes the stick in the ground and places the extra glove, pocket facing catcher, on top of the stick. She then positions herself behind the glove/stick target. The glove should be about two feet above the ground.

The procedure is the same as in "Percentage Throw," except Player 1 retrieves all throws and awards points accordingly. The catcher earns two points for balls that either hit the glove, stick, or come close enough to throw out a runner. Player 1 acts as judge.

Watch for these common errors:

- Improper grip (ball tails or sails away from target).
- Throwing arm brought back too far.
- Ball released with a three-quarter or sidearm motion.

- Not releasing the ball with a quick overhand snap.
- Taking an extra step before releasing the ball.

Blocking Home Plate

- Give the runner part of the plate. This encourages the runner to slide away rather than into the catcher.
- Wait for the throw to reach the plate.
- Hold ball with right hand and cover it with the mitt.
- Drop to the left knee, apply a firm tag, and pull it away before the runner tries to kick ball out of the mitt. Try to take the throw on the third-base side of the plate. Tag runner with the back of the glove.
- If you must leave home plate to catch the ball, do so quickly, and attempt to tag out runner by sweeping mitt toward the third-base side of home plate.

Have your catcher, wearing full equipment, stand behind home plate while you walk out to the mound. Tell catcher to tag out an imaginary runner as you throw her the ball. Repeat several times pointing out any problems that develop.

Now liven up the drill by having a player act as runner. Send runner to third base. On "Go," have runner, wearing safety helmet, attempt to beat the tag at home. Time your throw to give catcher a chance to set herself at home plate. Make an occasional bad throw to force the catcher to come out and meet the ball. If she has a play at home, she should try to tag the runner with a sweeping motion of her mitt and hand. If not, she should simulate a throw to a base where she might put out a runner.

Watch for these common errors:

- Attempting to tag out runner before catching ball or setting self for collision.
- Blocking off home plate encouraging runner to collide with catcher.
- Goes after runner (doesn't let runner "tag herself out").
- Tags runner with front of mitt.
- Goes out after ball and then tries to come back for the tag.
- Remains at home plate and tries to catch wildly thrown ball.

Fielding Bunts

- Explode out of the chute.
- Scoop up ball with mitt and bare hand.
- Face in the direction you will make your throw.
- Bring ball back to throwing position.

Have your basemen go to their positions. Go to the mound and send your catcher behind home plate.

Alternate rolling "bunts" down the first and third base lines. Call out the base you want the catcher to make her throw.

On throws to first base, have catcher throw to the inside of the diamond. This will prevent the baseman from colliding with the runner. On balls rolling down the third baseline, have catcher charge to her left, scoop up the ball, and move toward the base where the throw will go.

Watch for these common errors:

- Not getting a good jump from home plate.
- Fielding the bunt with one hand.
- Lifting the head and pulling eyes away from the ball before fielding it.
- Keeping body weight over back foot.

Catching Fly Balls

- Come to a standing position immediately.
- Locate the ball, remove the face mask, and toss it in the opposite direction. Pop flies around home plate tend to drift toward the infield.
- Position yourself under the ball. Line ball up with top of head.
- Flex knees and keep weight over the toes. If the ball is hit directly up over the plate, go out in front with back to the infield.
- Catch ball in front of face (Figure 2.4).

INDIVIDUAL DRILLS FOR CATCHERS

The following individual drills are designed to help athletes master basic skills necessary to be a successful catcher.

Wrist Flip

Purpose: To snap the ball forward quickly.

Figure 2.4

Hold mitt out in front of body even with waist. Grip the ball across the seams. Cock the ball at the ear. Now snap the ball forward by pushing hard with the index and middle finger, whipping the wrist downward. A fast, strong wrist snap will cause the ball to hit the mitt with a loud popping sound.

Accurate Throw

Purpose: To make accurate overhand throws.

Tape a target (cardboard, towel, etc.) about three feet off the ground against a garage door or solid wall. Stand about 30 feet away from the structure and throw a soft rubber ball at the target until your arm warms. Then step back ten feet for every six throws at the target. Continue to throw until you are approximately 90 feet away. Make mental notes at what distance you showed the greatest throwing accuracy. Now ask yourself these questions:

1. Did I hold the ball with a cross-seam grip?
2. As I brought the ball back to my ear, did I keep my weight on the back foot?
3. Did I shift weight from my right to my left foot as I started to throw?

4. Did I point my left foot toward the target?

5. Did I follow through completely by shifting weight to the left foot and bringing the right arm over and down?

6. Did I snap the wrists straight downward?

Shifting Feet

Purpose: To practice shifting the feet to the left and to the right.

Go to an open area or garage or backyard. Assume a receiving stance. Imagine the pitcher throwing an inside pitch (to a right-hander). Shift the left foot, catch the ball, and simulate a return throw. Return to a receiving stance. "See" the pitcher throwing an outside pitch. Shift the right foot, catch the ball, and simulate a return throw.

Alternate shifting one foot or taking one step while shifting both feet at the same time.

Pop Fly

Purpose: To practice catching pop flies in front of the face.

Bring a catcher's mask, mitt, and softball to an open area. Put on the mask. Toss the ball high into air with an underhand throw. As soon as you release the ball, count off one second. Then look up, locate the ball, and toss the mask in the opposite direction with your bare hand. Line up the ball with the top of your head and catch it in front of your face.

On windy days, test wind direction and speed by tossing grass into the air and adjust accordingly.

Scoop and Throw

Purpose: To practice scooping up the ball with mitt and bare hand.

Go to an open area and place three softballs on the ground about 15 feet in front of you. Set Ball One to the left, Ball Two to the right, and Ball Three directly out in front.

Assume a crouching stance. Then fire out, think "play at first," and surround Ball 1. Turn your body toward first base, scoop up the ball with mitt and bare hand, and simulate a throw.

Repeat the procedure. Think "play at third" for Ball 2 and "play at second" for Ball 3. Field and "throw" until you are satisfied with your performance.

SMALL-GROUP DRILLS FOR CATCHERS

Two, three, or four athletes participate in the following drills. Whenever possible, allow pitchers and catchers to work together. The length of each drill is subject to coach's discretion.

Two-Player Drills

One-Hopper

Catcher and partner go to an open area. The catcher wears protective equipment, including face mask, and assumes her catching position. Partner stands about 40 feet away and throws one-hoppers to the left, to the right, and directly in front of the catcher. The catcher doesn't try to catch the ball, she uses her body to keep the ball from getting past her.

Partner Should Watch for These Errors:

- Catcher isn't low enough; she's leaving the gate open. Correction: Have her sit on her heels.

- Weight not forward, hands spread apart. Correction: Have her lean forward and keep both hands inside her thighs.

- Catcher unable to stop balls thrown to the side. Correction: Have her concentrate on keeping her body in line with the ball.

Throw/Go

Catcher and partner go to an open area. Partner and catcher stand about 80 feet apart and face each other. Partner places two softballs about 20 feet apart in a straight line between herself and the catcher. The catcher assumes a crouching stance.

Partner shouts, "Go," catcher fires out, scoops up the first ball, and makes an overhand throw to partner. She then fields the second ball and makes another overhand throw. After the second throw, catcher turns around and sprints away from her partner. Partner yells "fly" and throws a high fly ball into the air. As soon as the catcher fields the ball and makes a return throw, partner tosses a second ball into the air. Catcher fields and makes a return throw.

Partner should watch for these errors:

- Catcher off balance when fielding pop flies. Correction: Have catcher line ball up with the top of her head.

- Catcher holds mitt too low when fielding pop flies. Correction: Have catcher field pop flies in front of her face.

- Catcher's throw tends to sail or tail away. Correction: Remind catcher to use a cross-seam grip and throw the ball overhand.
- Catcher makes wild throws. Correction: Remind catcher to throw overhand with a complete follow-through.

Roll/Throw/Go

The procedure is the same for "Throw/Go" with one exception: Partner doesn't place balls, she tosses two buntlike balls, one at a time, to the left and to the right of the catcher. Partner waits until catcher fields and throws the first ball before she tosses the second ball.

Partner should watch for these errors:

- Catcher fields with one hand. Correction: Insist that catcher fields ball with mitt and bare hand.
- Catcher throws off target. Correction: Have catcher turn in direction of target as she scoops the ball and make an overhand throw.

Three-Player Drills

Hustle

Catcher and two players bring two movable rubber bases to an open area. The bases represent first and third. Player 1, tosser, stands about 40 feet away from Player 2, catcher. Player 3, fielder, stands near first base.

Player 1, acting as pitcher, begins action by rolling a slow bouncer to the left of Player 2. Player 2 charges, scoops up the ball, and throws it to Player 3. She then sprints to third base, touches it, turns around, and heads back to her starting position. Player 3 yells "pop up" and throws a high fly into the air. After releasing the ball, Player 3 runs to third base and stops. Player 1 helps Player 2 line up the catch by shouting instructions; for example, "to the left," "to the right," and so on. When Player 2 catches the ball, she turns toward third and makes an overhand throw.

On the Go

Catcher and two players bring two movable rubber bases and three softballs to an open area. The bases act as first and second.

Player 1, retriever, stands about 40 feet away from Player 2, catcher. Player 3, fielder, stands near first base. Player 1 sets three softballs in a V pattern between Player 2 and Player 3 (Figure 2.5).

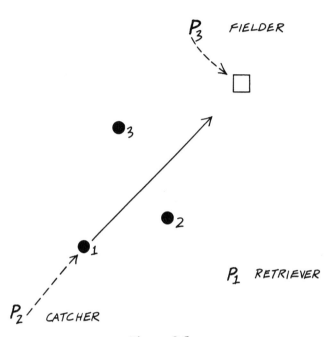

Figure 2.5

Player 2 assumes a catching stance. Action begins when Player 1 hollers "go." Player 2 charges, scoops up Ball 1, and throws it to Player 3.

Player 1 replaces the balls and the drill is repeated. This time Player 3 moves to second base to take the throws.

Four-Player Drills

Fire Away

Three players and a catcher go to the diamond. The catcher sets a ball on the ground between home plate and the mound. Players act as basemen and take their positions.

The catcher assumes a crouching stance behind home plate. Action begins when the catcher fires out, scoops up the ball, and throws to a baseman. The first baseman waits until the catcher touches a ball before she shouts "first," "second," or "third." The catcher makes an overhand throw to the indicated baseman.

The baseman waits until the catcher returns to her crouch position before she tosses a slow bouncer toward the catcher. The baseman hollers "first," "second," or "third" as the catcher touches the ball.

The catcher should continue play until she fields at least nine balls or throws to each base three times.

Block Her

Three players and a catcher go to the diamond. Two players, wearing helmets, go to third base and act as runners. One player goes to the mound and becomes the tosser. Catcher, wearing full equipment, takes a crouching position behind home plate.

Action begins when the tosser yells "go" and the first runner in line breaks toward home. When the runner is about half way down the line, tosser throws the ball to the catcher. Catcher attempts to tag out runner. The tosser should vary her throws—inside low, high outside, one hoppers—to make the drill more challenging. Runners should slide on every play.

Catcher should concentrate on:

- Tagging runner with back side of glove.
- Planting left foot firmly, then reaching for the ball, and swinging back for the tag.
- Trying to take the throw on the third base side of the plate.
- Using both hands when tagging the runner.
- Leaving the plate to take throws *only* when absolutely necessary.

TIPS AND SUGGESTIONS
FOR THE CATCHER

Pass along the following information to your catchers:

1. Study the batter. Look for her weakness and set target accordingly.
2. Keep your pitcher sharp. Talk to her between innings. Go over individual batting weaknesses and set a plan of attack.

3. Let teammates know you're alive and well. Continually shout out words of encouragement to your pitcher and team members.

4. Keep your head in the game. Move players around or help them make adjustments when certain hitters come to the plate. For example, if you know the batter (right-hander) pulls the ball, signal players to shift to the left side.

5. Be enthusiastic, determined, and aggressive. Your behavior helps set the mood for the game.

6. Hustle, hustle, hustle. Let everyone know you came to play.

7. Keep signals simple and give your pitcher a clear target.

8. Watch the pitcher for signs of fatigue or frustration. A struggling pitcher who loses her composure cripples her team's chance of winning.

9. Don't reach to the sides to catch the ball. Move out quickly and bring your body in front of the ball.

10. Block balls thrown in the dirt with your body. Don't try to catch them.

11. Make all throws with an overhand motion and complete follow-through. Try to hit the baseman with a waist-high, glove-side throw.

12. Get rid of the ball quickly. Don't take an extra step or two before releasing the ball.

13. Give pitcher a still target. Avoid bouncing around behind home plate.

14. Call all infield plays for pop flies, bunts, and foul balls.

POINTS TO REMEMBER

The catcher must be active behind home plate, direct traffic on the field, and keep the pace of the game moving at a steady clip.

A good catcher seldom relaxes. She's constantly studying each hitter and watching the other players throughout the game.

An effective catcher must know how to handle pitchers, have the ability to lead, and be able to instill confidence in others. She should have quick hands and quick feet, make strong, accurate throws, and be able to catch any kind of pitch.

3. First Base

A SPORTSWRITER ONCE WROTE in his column that his grandmother could play first base. The truth, of course, is that a first baseman plays a significant role in the success of her team. After all, the first baseman handles more chances than any fielder except the catcher.

A first baseman should be fairly tall and have the ability to stop wild throws coming from all directions. She must be able to shift her feet quickly, stop hard hit balls, and make accurate throws around the infield.

We'll cover these topics in this section:

1. Preparing the first baseman for competition
2. Examining the mechanics of playing first base
3. Individual drills for the first baseman
4. Drills for two or more players
5. Tips and suggestions for the first baseman
6. Points to remember

PREPARING THE FIRST BASEMAN
FOR COMPETITION

A first baseman stretches and jumps like an acrobat when she catches thrown balls. She constantly shifts her feet around the bag and positions her body to prevent wild throws from getting past her.

Pass along these three stretching exercises to help ready your first baseman for action:

1. Lay a glove or ball on the ground. Stand directly over it with your legs spread about four feet apart. Slowly lower your body by bending at the knees and waist. Try to touch the object with your knees and elbows. Hold position for ten seconds. Return to ready position and repeat six or eight times.

2. Stand erect, feet shoulder width apart. Place hands on hips. Slowly reach down with both hands and touch the toes. Then jump straight up reaching as high as possible. Return to starting position and repeat six or eight times.

3. Plant your right foot on the ground, keeping knees straight. Step ahead with your left foot as far as possible. Rest both hands on your left knee and bend forward. Hold this position for five seconds. Repeat five times with each leg. This exercise stretches the calf muscle, or the fleshy part of the leg below the knee.

EXAMINING THE MECHANICS
OF PLAYING FIRST BASE

Once a player learns how to shift her feet around the bag she will relax and feel comfortable playing first base.

On a ground ball hit to an infielder, the first baseman races to the bag and turns to the infielder making the throw. She keeps both feet inside the bag with heels practically touching it and takes a long stride reaching as far as possible. She keeps the toe of her left foot (left-handed player) pressed against the side of the bag and extends her right foot.

Often an extended stretch nips the runner by a half step. This extra effort tests the determination and agility of the first baseman.

You can help the first baseman improve her stretching by having her go to the bag, assume her fielding position, and break for the base on the command "Go." Tell her to find the bag, turn toward you, and stretch out. Make a mark in the dirt below her glove to show the length of her reach.

Repeat the procedure. This time toss a ball hard enough to reach the mark, but one requiring the baseman to fully extend herself. Tell her not to stretch too soon or she'll be unable to change direction if a throw is off target.

Shifting Feet

For throws coming to the left side of the bag, the baseman touches the base with her right foot and stretches with her left. For throws coming to the right side of the bag, the baseman touches the base with her left foot and stretches with her right.

Receiving Throws

A first baseman may have to leave the bag to take a throw. A novice player makes the mistake of staying on the base instead of catching the ball first, then going for the bag.

A first baseman must be adept at catching balls thrown low or in the dirt. She must learn early to block balls with her body if she can't field on the short hop. The idea, of course, is to keep the ball in front of her.

The first baseman must jump for high throws, catch the ball, and tag the runner in one quick, sweeping motion. A late tag or late jump may cause the first baseman to bobble the ball or miss tagging the runner. An anxious first baseman often attempts to tag the runner before she catches the ball.

A smart first baseman will give an inside target for all throws coming from home plate. A first baseman can handle an inside throw without risking a collision with the runner.

Fielding

The bounce throw is one of the most difficult plays a first baseman can make. She has to decide quickly whether to hold her position or back up to field the ball. If the throw hits the dirt well in front of the bag, the baseman should back up, field the ball on the foul side of first base, and tag the bag with the nearest foot.

Factors such as game situation, fielding ability, and knowledge of the hitter determine how far off the bag a baseman should play. Here are four key points to give your first baseman in regard to fielding:

1. Stay low as you go. Keep body weight shifted slightly forward and over the toes. Keep feet shoulder width apart and bend at the knees and waist (Figure 3.1).

2. Face the batter. Hold arms out in front of your body, touching glove hand to the ground.

3. Talk to the pitcher and second baseman. Plan your fielding strategy ahead of time.

4. Expect every ball to be hit to you.

Figure 3.1

On balls hit to the right of the mound, the pitcher breaks for first. The baseman fields and tosses the ball to the pitcher. The throw must be hard enough to reach the pitcher at least two steps ahead of the runner.

How a baseman covers the bunt is determined by coaching philosophy. You may want her to charge quickly, field, and throw according to directions given by the catcher, or stay close to the bag. The baseman should cover first on balls bunted down the third base line.

INDIVIDUAL DRILLS FOR THE FIRST BASEMAN

A first baseman can work on these drills during practice or at home:

Rebound

Stand about 30 feet away from a wall. Toss a rubber ball or tennis ball against the wall and field the rebound. Visualize a fielder throwing the ball to you. Adjust the distance and speed of the throw to get the desired return.

Practice fielding single-bounce or shoetop returns and wide rebounds. A thrown ball that hits the ground before striking the wall will come back as a high lob. Alternate throwing a rubber ball and tennis ball.

After throwing several balls overhand, switch to three-quarter and sidearm deliveries. This helps prepare the arm for making various throws.

Stretch

Go to an open area and set up a base target (board, cushion, etc.). Come off the bag, take a fielding stance facing home plate, and stay low. Visualize a batter hitting a ball to the third baseman. Break for the bag, find the infield side of the base with heel, turn toward the throw, and stretch out for the catch.

Practice shifting feet until it becomes automatic. Let's review footwork:

Right-Hander. For throws to the left, place right foot on infield side of bag, stretch with left foot (Figure 3.2). For throws to the right, place left foot on outfield side of bag, stretch with right foot (Figure 3.3). A first baseman may wish to use her right foot to tag the base on all throws. No problem here as long as she makes the putout.

Left-Hander. For throws to the left, place right foot on infield side of bag, stretch with left foot. For throws to the right, place left foot on inside of bag, stretch with right foot (Figure 3.4).

Figure 3.2

Figure 3.3

Figure 3.4

Charge

Go to an open area. Set a ball on the ground and stand about 30 feet away. Assume a low fielding stance facing the ball. Visualize a batter bunting the ball. Charge quickly, think "first," "second," or "third," pick up the ball, and simulate a throw in that direction.

Repeat procedure. Alternate simulating throws to first, second, and third.

DRILLS FOR TWO OR MORE PLAYERS

Glove Up, Glove Down

Purpose: To practice turning the glove in the right direction.

The first baseman and a partner go to an open area. They stand about 30 feet apart. Partner begins action by tossing the ball, three-quarter speed, to the first baseman. She alternates throwing knee-high and shoulder-high deliveries. Have partner check to see that the first baseman catches balls above her waist by holding the glove-pocket side down. For balls thrown below her waist, she should hold the glove-pocket side up.

Leave the Base

Purpose: To practice leaving the base to catch off-target throws.

The first baseman and a partner bring a movable rubber base to an open area. They stand about 30 feet apart. Partner begins action by tossing high outside or low inside throws to the first baseman forcing her to leave the base. Have partner check to see that the first baseman catches the ball first before attempting to tag the bag.

Charge and Throw

Purpose: To practice charging the ball quickly and making accurate throws.

Three players bring a movable rubber base to an open area. Player 1 acts as catcher, Player 2 as fielder, and Player 3 takes first base.

Action begins when Player 1 hollers "Go" and tosses a slow roller onto the infield. The first baseman charges, fields, and throws to Player 2 covering first base. The first baseman concentrates on making chest-high, glove-side throws to the inside of the baseline.

Play continues as the first baseman makes three throws to first, second, and third respectively. Player 2 receives the throws and returns the ball to Player 1.

Underhand Toss

Purpose: To practice making underhand tosses to the pitcher covering first.

Three players (two pitchers and a baseman) bring a movable rubber base to an open area. Player 1 acts as catcher, Player 2 as pitcher, and Player 3 takes first base. Player 1 and Player 2 trade off at their positions.

Action begins when Player 1 tosses a hard grounder to the left of Player 2. Player 2 breaks for first by running at a slight angle to the baseline. Then when she is about three feet from the line, she should cut sharply to her left and run parallel to the baseline. This will prevent her from colliding with the runner in a game situation. The baseman makes an underhand, chest-high toss at least two steps ahead of Player 2. If the baseman goes to her far right to field the ball, she should make an overhand throw to Player 2.

Finding the Range

Purpose: To determine the fielding range of the first baseman.

Three players bring a movable rubber base to an open area. Player 1 acts as catcher, Player 2 as the second baseman, and Player 3 takes first base.

Action begins as Player 1 tosses a hard grounder to the right of Player 3. Player 3 fields and returns the ball to Player 1. Player 2 backs up Player 3. Action continues with Player 1 making each successive throw harder to field. When Player 3 can no longer go to her right and field the ball, play stops. The first baseman places a marker —stick or towel—about ten feet in front of her to indicate how far she can extend herself and successfully field the ball. The drill continues as Player 1 throws a variety of ground balls between the marker and first base.

In the Middle

Purpose: To practice catching and blocking the ball.

Three players go to an open area. Player 1 and Player 2 stand about 30 feet apart and face each other. Player 3, first baseman, stands between them and assumes a low-fielding position.

Action begins when Player 1 throws a ball at the first baseman. The throw may be on target, in the dirt, wild high, or to the side. The first baseman must try to stop the ball any way she can. Player 1 can fake before throwing or do anything tricky to throw the first baseman off-balance. If the first baseman catches or blocks the ball, she must throw it to Player 2. Player 2 follows the same procedure.

The drill becomes lively when Player 1 teams up with Player 2 to outwit the baseman. For instance, Player 2 can use finger signals to indicate where she wants Player 1 to throw the ball. The throw, however, should be within the fielding range of the baseman.

TIPS AND SUGGESTIONS
FOR THE FIRST BASEMAN

The following information will help keep the first baseman sharp and ready to compete.

1. Know what to do with the ball at all times. Think ahead.

2. Coordinate strategy with teammates. Know the limits of your ability and those of your team members.

3. Stay natural. Don't force yourself to do anything that will negatively affect your performance.

4. Seek improvement through consistent practice. Use visualization techniques to see yourself as a success.

5. Be an aggressive fielder. Charge hard, stay low, and come up throwing.

6. Whenever possible, use two hands to catch the ball.

7. Work closely with the catcher on bunt situations. She will tell you where to throw the ball.

8. Listen to your coach. Leave yourself open for constructive criticism.

POINTS TO REMEMBER

A tall, rangy left-hander has the advantage over a short right-handed player. But size alone does not a first baseman make. An athlete with a small stature can become a superior first baseman through desire and determination.

If an athlete, regardless of size, has her heart set on playing first base, she has the battle half-won. Now all she has to do is catch everything thrown at her, field aggressively, and make accurate throws. Again, these skills can be developed through intensive practice.

4. Second Base

THE SECOND BASEMAN should be an excellent fielder with sure hands. She should be able to move quickly to her right and left, throw from any position, and catch high pop-ins in the infield.

This chapter will cover these topics:

1. Preparing the second baseman for action
2. Examining the mechanics of playing second base
3. Individual drills for the second baseman
4. Drills and activities for two or more players
5. Tips and suggestions for the second baseman
6. Points to remember

PREPARING THE SECOND BASEMAN FOR ACTION

Since the second baseman is constantly moving about and changing directions, she should concentrate on stretching her arm and leg muscles. Simple stretching exercises like toe-touches, back-arches, and sit-ups should do the job.

Some ballplayers react slowly to balls hit to the right or left. They either get a poor jump on the ball or fail to make an accurate throw after fielding the ball. The problem usually occurs when the second baseman throws her balance off by keeping body weight shifted over her heels, or by staying high while trying to field and throw.

If your second baseman needs work in this area, have her try the following:

- Assume a low fielding position, glove touching ground.
- Keep body weight shifted over toes, arms extended out in front of body.
- Break to the right, field an imaginary ball by planting right foot, and make a simulated overhand throw to first.
- Alternate fielding to the right and left. Repeat six times.

Now ask your second baseman to imagine fielding a ball hit to her far right and far left. This time have her reach out by extending her glove hand, put on the brakes, set herself, and turn and throw.

Add a touch of realism. Go to first base and toss grounders to the second baseman's right and left. Have her concentrate on making chest-high, glove-side throws. After she fields six or eight balls, go to third base and continue play. Remind player to stay low and keep her body in front of the ball.

EXAMINING THE MECHANICS OF PLAYING SECOND BASE

Pass these tips along to your second baseman:

Fielding (Bases Empty)

Balls Hit Directly at the Baseman

- Stay low. Field ball off of right foot, keeping body in front of ball (Figure 4.1).
- Maintain body weight over toes, feet spread shoulder width apart.

Balls Hit to the Right

- Stay low. Get to the ball quickly.
- Field the ball, put on the brakes (come to a full stop), straighten up, and throw.

Balls Hit to the Left

- Stay low. Get to the ball quickly.
- Field the ball and make throw while moving toward first base.

Pop Flies Hit into Shallow Right Field

- Spot ball. Turn and run into short right field.
- Call for the ball. Make catch while facing the infield, if possible.

Figure 4.1

Throwing

The game situation, ball speed, and direction determine the kind of throw a second baseman makes. Without a doubt, she must be able to throw from any position. A smart second baseman will spend time in practice making three-quarter, sidearm, and underhand tosses.

Starting a Double Play

On balls hit near the bag, the baseman fields on the run and makes a simple underhand toss to the glove side of the shortstop covering the base. Tell her to make a chest-high toss with the palm facing second base. Also, ask her to give the shortstop a clear view of the ball.

As a pivot man in a double play, have the second baseman touch the outfield side of the bag, step backward and to the side, and throw to first (Figure 4.2). On throws to the inside of the base, tag the bag, move toward the mound, and throw to first (Figure 4.3).

Figure 4.2a

Figure 4.2b

Figure 4.2c

Figure 4.3

The pivot may be a difficult maneuver for the second baseman to learn. Perhaps the best thing to do is show your second baseman various pivots to the left and to the right; then have her team up with the shortstop and decide which pivoting techniques work best for both of them.

Offer these hints to the second baseman:

- Get to the bag quickly.
- Stay on balance. Be ready to take the throw, tag the bag, and shift in any direction for the throw.
- Keep your eyes fixed on your target—the first baseman.

Tagging the Base Runners

On a steal the second baseman straddles the bag, fields the throw, and tags the runner with the back of her glove. A runner should be allowed to tag herself out. After making the tag, bring hands back quickly.

INDIVIDUAL DRILLS FOR THE SECOND BASEMAN

Here are three drills that help an athlete prepare mentally and physically for playing second base. Each drill requires the baseman to bring two movable rubber bases to an open area.

Pivoting

Set two bases—first and second—about 40 feet apart. Assume a fielding position. Break quickly for second, take an imaginary throw from the shortstop, tag the base, and throw to first.

Repeat the procedure. This time break to the left or right, field an imaginary ball, and throw to the shortstop breaking across the bag.

Covering First

Set two bases—first and second—about 40 feet apart. Assume a fielding position. Visualize a batter bunting the ball. Break for first, touch the base, and give an inside target by stretching toward the mound.

High Fly

Set two bases—first and second—about 40 feet apart. Assume a fielding position. Visualize a towering pop fly drifting into shallow right or center field. Turn, run to where you think the ball will land, look up, locate and catch the ball.

An athlete can combine all three drills and complete the series in 15 minutes or less. The effectiveness of these activities hinges on an athlete's determination to improve her skills without actually handling the ball.

DRILLS AND ACTIVITIES FOR TWO OR MORE PLAYERS

The second baseman and a partner can work the individual drills outlined in the previous section. The partner, acting as tosser, throws the ball to the second baseman in each activity.

The following five drills require movable rubber bases, up to four softballs, and a shortstop.

Four to Six, Six to Four

Two players—second baseman and shortstop—bring a movable rubber base and four softballs to an open area. The rubber base acts as second. The players take their positions, and balls are placed on the ground according to Figure 4.4. Balls should be spaced about 20 feet apart.

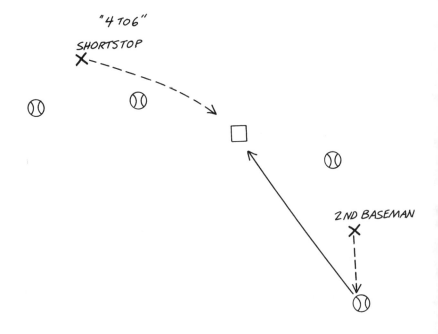

Figure 4.4

Action begins when the shortstop yells "Four to Six." The second baseman breaks either left or right, scoops up the ball, and throws it to the shortstop covering second. After catching the ball and tagging the base, the shortstop replaces the ball and returns to her position. Play continues as the second baseman shouts "Six to Four." The shortstop breaks either left or right, scoops up the ball, and throws it to the second baseman covering the bag. After catching the ball and tagging the base, the second baseman replaces the ball and returns to her position.

Athletes alternate breaking to the left and right. Each player can help one another by pointing out problem areas and ways to correct them.

A third player, coach or infielder, can liven up the drill by hitting ground balls to each infielder. She keeps the fielders on their toes by hollering "Four to Six" or "Six to Four" moments before hitting the ball.

Dead Ball, Live Ball

Three players—second baseman, shortstop, and tosses—bring a movable rubber base (second) and three softballs to an open area. The players take their positions and balls are placed on the ground according to Figure 4.5.

Action begins when the tosser hollers "Six Right." The shortstop breaks to her right, fields the ball, and throws to the second baseman covering the bag. She then breaks toward second, fields a grounder thrown by the tosser, and throws to the second baseman. The second baseman replaces the resting ball and throws the second ball back to the tosser. Both fielders return to their original positions. Play continues as the tosser hollers "Four Left." The second baseman breaks to her left, fields the ball, and throws to the shortstop covering the bag. She then breaks toward second, fields a grounder thrown by the tosser, and throws to the shortstop. The shortstop replaces the resting ball and throws the second ball back to the tosser. Both fielders return to their original positions.

The tosser controls the pace of the drill by varying the speed and direction of ground balls. Again, athletes should monitor each other's progress and make necesary corrections.

Underhand Toss Game

Three players—shortstop, second baseman, and tosser—bring a movable rubber base (second) and a softball to an open area. Athletes position themselves according to Figure 4.5.

Action starts when the tosser rolls a ball to the left of second, near the base, and yells "Shortstop." The shortstop breaks to her left,

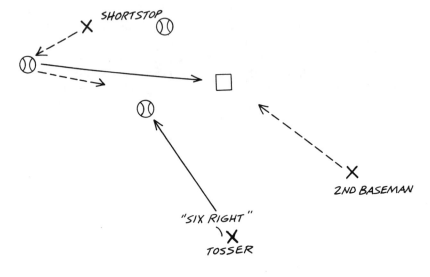

Figure 4.5

fields, and makes an underhand toss to the second baseman covering
the base. The second baseman straddles second and holds her glove
waist-high, pocket side up. She stands perfectly still unless she must
move or cover herself from being struck in the face with the ball.

The fielder scores points as follows:

- Ball hits glove and bounces away—1 point.
- Ball hits glove pocket and bounces away—2 points.
- Ball hits glove pocket and stays in the glove—3 points.

The shortstop fields and throws five times. Then she straddles
second while the second baseman fields and throws five times. The
player with the most points after three rounds (five balls per round)
wins. *Note:* The fielder, to be successful, must concentrate on making
easy, underhand tosses.

Straddle Throw Game

Three players—shortstop, second baseman, and tosser—bring a
movable rubber base (second) and a softball to an open area. Athletes
position themselves according to Figure 4.5.

Action begins when the shortstop straddles second base and
holds her glove about two feet above the base. The tosser flips a

grounder to the second baseman's right. The infielder breaks, fields, and makes a sidearm throw to the shortstop. The fielder earns points according to the scoring system in "Underhand Toss Game."

After throwing the ball, the second baseman returns to her position. The tosser flips a grounder to the second baseman's left. The second baseman breaks, fields, and comes to a complete stop. She sets herself and makes an overhand or three-quarter throw to the shortstop. After fielding three balls to the left and to the right, athletes switch off. The second baseman straddles the bag and the shortstop fields. The player with the most points after two rounds (six balls per round) wins.

Dead Center

Three players—shortstop, second baseman, and tosser—bring a movable rubber base (second) and a softball to an open area. Athletes position themselves according to Figure 4.5.

Action starts when the tosser yells "Break" and bounces a grounder between the shortstop and second baseman. The tosser then hollers "Shortstop" or "Second" to indicate which player should field the ball. *Note:* The fielder must do everything possible to stop the ball, pick it up, and make a throw to the tosser covering second base. The tosser can make the drill more challenging by having the fielders play deeper than normal. The tosser controls the pace of the drill by varying ball speed.

TIPS AND SUGGESTIONS FOR THE SECOND BASEMAN

Pass along the following information to your second baseman:

1. Keep your head in the ballgame at all times. Your coach and teammates expect you to stay alert and make quick decisions.
2. Get to know the shortstop, her moves, and how she thinks. Your effectiveness, especially when executing the double play, will depend on how well you and the shortstop work together.
3. Be involved in every play. There is always something to do. A hustling second baseman makes the infield come alive.
4. Hang tough when attempting difficult maneuvers. Just keep practicing until you feel comfortable with the results.

POINTS TO REMEMBER

An alert second baseman manages to be in the right place at the right time. She also times her throwing and fielding moves to match those of the shortstop when executing the double play.

An agile second baseman has the flexibility to throw from nearly any position. Her ability to get to the ball quickly and make accurate throws often determines the direction of the game.

5. Shortstop

A GIRL WITH A STRONG, accurate arm may do well playing shortstop. She should be fast afoot, able to move quickly to the left and right, and make long throws to first base. Since the shortstop fields more ground balls than any other infielder, she should be an excellent fielder.

We'll examine these areas in this chapter:

1. Preparing the shortstop for action
2. Examining the mechanics of playing shortstop
3. Individual drills for the shortstop
4. Drills and activities for two or more players
5. Tips and suggestions for the shortstop
6. Points to remember

PREPARING THE SHORTSTOP FOR ACTION

The warm-up session should include plenty of stretching and bending exercises. Since the shortstop covers a wide range of territory, she should practice getting a good jump forward, backward, and to her left and right.

Warming the throwing arm before attempting long, hard throws is imperative. The shortstop must make accurate sidearm, underhand, or overhand tosses. Therefore, she should spend 15 to 20 minutes loosening her arm muscles. After five minutes of throwing, have the shortstop gradually increase the distance and speed of her throws.

EXAMINING THE MECHANICS OF PLAYING SHORTSTOP

Chapter 4 included several drills for both second basemen and shortstops. The activities stressed fielding, throwing, and executing the double play. Let's study the shortstop as she throws the ball and acts as pivot man on the double play.

Making Throws

On balls hit near the base, the shortstop should make an easy underhand throw to the second baseman. Have her lead the second baseman with a chest-high toss.

There is no ironclad rule for throwing the ball. However, when the play goes to first base, you should encourage your shortstop to throw as follows:

Batted Ball	*Kind of Throw*
Regular ground ball	Overhand
Slow bounder or high chopper	Overhand, sidearm, or underhand (depending on speed and location of ball)

All long throws to any base should be made with an overhand motion. Again, the secret is getting to the ball quickly and making a strong throw with a complete follow-through.

Pivot Position on the Double Play

As the pivot man on double-play situations, the shortstop can tag the bag in several ways. Here are three easy moves you can teach your shortstop:

1. *Bag Tag:* Move toward the bag, take throw from second, and tag bag with left foot. Then step back from bag and throw (Figure 5.1).

2. *Left Step:* Move toward the bag, take throw from second, and step on bag with left foot. Swing right foot behind left, plant right foot, and throw (Figure 5.2).

3. *Drag Right Foot:* Move toward the bag, take throw from second, and drag right foot across base. Step out of the base path with the left foot, hop to the right, and throw (Figure 5.3).

Figure 5.1a

Figure 5.1b

Figure 5.2a

Figure 5.2b

Figure 5.3a

Figure 5.3b

INDIVIDUAL DRILLS FOR THE SHORTSTOP

The following three drills stress fielding, throwing, and covering second on the double-play situation. Give them to your shortstop so she can practice on her own.

Any Direction

Set four softballs in a diamond pattern surrounding you. Stand in the middle of the pattern. Each ball should be about 20 feet away from you. Assume a fielding position, glove touching the ground. Begin action in this manner:

- Break to your left, field ball, and simulate a sidearm throw to first. Replace ball. Return to starting position.
- Break to your right, field ball, and simulate an overhand throw to first. Replace ball. Return to starting position.
- Break straight ahead, field ball, and simulate a sidearm flip to first. Replace ball. Return to starting position.
- Turn around, field ball with back facing first, spin around, and simulate an overhand throw to first. Replace ball. Return to starting position. Repeat the procedure. Now do this:

- Field to the left, simulate an underhand toss to second.
- Field to the right, simulate a sidearm throw to second.
- Break straight ahead, simulate a sidearm throw to second.
- Turn around, simulate a sidearm throw to second. Try to complete circuit in 30 seconds or less. Repeat four or five times.

Chest High

Tape a cloth target (12 inch square) about chest-high on a wall or garage door. Stand about 40 or 50 feet away and throw a soft rubber ball against the wall.

If you field the rebound to your right, make a sidearm or overhand throw at the target. If the rebound comes to your left, make a sidearm throw at the target. If the ball comes straight at you, make a sidearm flip at the target.

To add interest, award yourself one point every time the ball strikes the target. Then score as follows:

- 7 points per 10 rebounds—outstanding, but not perfect. Keep practicing.
- 5 points per 10 rebounds—average, but not outstanding. Practice some more.
- 3 points per 10 rebounds—poor, far from average. Practice, practice, practice.

In short, unless you can hit the target *every* time, continue to concentrate and work hard.

Middle Man

Bring a movable rubber base to an open area. Assume a low fielding position, glove touching the ground.

Visualize the second baseman fielding a ground ball with a runner at first. Break toward the bag, catch the toss from the second baseman, tag the bag, and throw to first.

Practice the three suggested techniques listed in this chapter or pick one that works best for you. During a game, the second baseman should know which maneuver you prefer in certain situations. This includes covering the base on steals and cut-off or relay responsibilities on balls hit into the outfield. A last-minute change creates confusion and upsets timing.

DRILLS AND ACTIVITIES FOR
TWO OR MORE PLAYERS

The shortstop and a partner take part in the following two drills:

Action Throw

Shortstop and partner (tosser) bring their gloves and a ball to an open area. Athletes stand about 50 feet apart and face each other.

Player 1, shortstop, acts as fielder. Player 2, tosser, throws the ball to the shortstop. Action begins when Player 2 tosses a grounder to the shortstop's right and hollers "sidearm" or "overhand." The shortstop fields, sets herself, and makes the designated chest-high throw to Player 2.

The tosser mixes sending grounders to the left, right, and directly in front of Player 1. The tosser may send Player 1 deep by throwing a high fly ball into the air. Player 2 keeps the drill alive by varying the speed and direction of the thrown ball.

After eight minutes or so, athletes should switch roles; that is, Player 1 becomes tosser and Player 2 fields the ball.

Covering Second

Shortstop and partner (second baseman) bring their gloves, a ball, and a movable rubber base to an open area. The base represents second. Athletes take their regular positions. Situation: Runner on first. Action begins when the second baseman tosses a grounder to shortstop, breaks for second, and gives a chest-high target with her glove. The shortstop fields and throws to the second baseman. If the ball is near the base, shortstop makes a soft, underhand throw to second. If the ball stays wide of the base or forces the shortstop to go deep, she should make a sidearm or overhand throw to the second baseman.

After fielding five balls, the shortstop becomes tosser and covers second while the second baseman fields and throws. Athletes should spend at least 15 minutes fielding and throwing.

Three athletes—a shortstop and two infielders—participate in the next two drills.

End of the Line

Shortstop and two infielders bring their gloves, a ball, and a movable rubber base to an open area. Athletes form a line and stand about 40 feet apart.

Player 1 stands behind the rubber base and acts as tosser. Player 2, shortstop, stays between Player 1 and Player 3.

Action begins when Player 1 tosses a grounder to the right or left of Player 2. Player 2 fields and makes a chest-high sidearm or overhand throw to Player 1 covering the base. After catching the ball, Player 1 makes a long overhand throw to Player 3. Player 2 runs to the base, turns around, and fields a throw by Player 3. Player 1 backs up the throw.

After the shortstop fields five times, athletes switch positions. Player 1 becomes Player 2, Player 2 becomes Player 3, and so on. Every athlete should field at least 15 balls.

Around

Shortstop and two other infielders bring their gloves and two balls to an open area. Athletes form a triangle and stand about 40 feet apart. The balls are placed about five feet apart in the center of the triangle. Player 1 stands at the west end of the triangle, Player 2 at the east end, and Player 3, shortstop, at the south end.

Action begins when Player 3 charges, picks up a ball, and makes a sidearm or overhand throw to Player 1. She then picks up the second ball and tosses it to Player 2. She immediately sprints back to her original position. Players 1 and 2, in turn, throw the ball to Player 3. After receiving each throw Player 3 simulates tagging out a sliding runner.

Player 3 replaces both balls and the drill continues with Player 2 charging a ball. Each athlete should repeat the procedure three times.

TIPS AND SUGGESTIONS FOR THE SHORTSTOP

Have your shortstop apply these guidelines during practice sessions and contests:

1. Make accurate, powerful throws. Stay in a low fielding position, ready to go left or right.
2. Play closer to third than second. It is easier for most shortstops to go left than right.
3. Get into the habit of backing up the third baseman when she fields the ball.
4. Concentrate on making chest-high throws to the baseman and catcher.

5. Position yourself to take relay throws from the outfield on balls going into left and center field. On base hits to right field with a runner at first, be ready to cut off the throw to third.

6. Stay alert during bunt situations. You'll need to cover second or third base if the baseman charges the ball.

7. On fly balls hit behind second base, both you and the second baseman run for it. If the baseman calls for the ball, you must race back to second and cover the bag. You may have a play at second base.

POINTS TO REMEMBER

The shortstop must prepare herself to field more ground balls than her teammates. She must adjust according to her speed, her agility, and the strength of her throwing arm.

It's important to have good lateral motion when breaking to the left and right. An effective shortstop gets to the ball quickly, sets herself, and makes accurate, chest-high throws.

6. Third Base

IT TAKES AN AGGRESSIVE athlete to play third base. She must take charge, block hardshots down the line with her body, and react quickly to high bouncers and bunted balls. The slow bouncer or bunt requires the third baseman to fire ahead and come up throwing.

Fast hands, a strong, accurate arm, and quick reactions are the main ingredients of a topnotch third baseman; she needs her quick reactions since she plays so close to the plate.

This section will include the following:

1. Preparing the third baseman for action
2. Examining the mechanics of playing third base
3. Individual drills for the third baseman
4. Drills and activities for two or more players
5. Tips and suggestions for the third baseman
6. Points to remember

PREPARING THE THIRD BASEMAN FOR ACTION

A ten- or fifteen-minute warm-up session involving stretching and bending exercises normally readies a third baseman for play.

After warming her throwing arm, she should make several underhand flips and sidearm tosses. Some third basemen practice getting a good jump by assuming a low fielding position and shifting body weight forward upon the toes, then breaking quickly to the left, right, or straight ahead for three or four steps.

EXAMINING THE MECHANICS OF PLAYING THIRD BASE

Fielding Position

The third baseman, like her fellow infielders, takes a low fielding position, touching her glove to the ground. She should keep her feet spread comfortably apart with body weight shifted over the toes. She may prefer to move her left foot slightly forward of her right foot. She then flexes her legs at the knees and extends her arms out in front of her body (Figure 6.1).

Figure 6.1

Charging the Slow Bouncer or Swinging Bunt

This is one of the toughest plays a third baseman will make. If the ball has stopped rolling, she must charge the ball, field it bare-handed, and throw underhand or sidearm to first. If the ball is still rolling we prefer to have the third baseman scoop the ball up with the glove and hand together and throw sidearm to first base. We prefer this method because of the size of the ball in comparison to the size of most girls' hands.

Give your third baseman these tips:

- Rush toward the ball. Scoop it up with your bare hand or glove and hand together.

- Make an underhand or sidearm throw to first base; your momentum forward will add power to the throw.

Stress these points:

- Watch the ball roll into your glove. Grip ball, then look at first and make a chest-high throw.
- If the ball stops rolling, push it into the ground to get a solid grip, and come up throwing.

Playing the Bunt

You must decide how you want your third baseman to play the bunt. For example, if the batter tries to move the runner from second to third, the third baseman would stay close to the bag. With runners on first and second, you might want the pitcher to charge the line and throw to the third baseman covering the bag. If the batter attempts to bring the runner from first to third, the third baseman may elect to charge or stay near the bag while the pitcher fields. If the third baseman charges, the catcher goes over to the bag, and the third baseman covers home.

INDIVIDUAL DRILLS FOR THE THIRD BASEMAN

These two drills stress getting a fast forward start and throwing on the run. Give them to your third baseman as part of her individual workout.

Single Ball

Bring a glove and ball to an open area. Set the ball on the ground, stand about 30 feet away, and assume a low fielding position. Charge the ball, grab it with your bare hand, push down hard to set the grip, and simulate an underhand or sidearm throw to first. Repeat three or four times.

Double Ball

Bring a glove and two balls to an open area. Place the balls in an east-west direction, four feet apart, and about 30 feet away from you. Assume a low fielding position. Repeat the same procedure outlined in "Single Ball." After simulating a throw, drop the ball, turn around, and charge the second ball. Replace both balls and repeat three or four times.

DRILLS AND ACTIVITIES FOR TWO OR MORE PLAYERS

Let your third baseman execute the following four drills with one or two partners:

Chest Block

Go to third base. Assume a low fielding position near the bag. Have a partner stand between home and third base and throw short hops straight at you. A short hop throw should bounce one or two feet in front of you.

Stay low. Keep your body in front of the ball and use your chest to knock the ball down. Pick up the ball and make a chest-high throw to your partner. Get into the habit of watching the ball carefully. Field and throw eight or ten times before switching.

Rollers

Repeat the procedure for "Chest Block." This time have your partner stand near home plate and toss slow rollers down the line, to the left of the bag, and straight ahead. Fire out, field barehanded, and toss the ball underhand or sidearm. After fielding and throwing eight or ten times, switch with your partner.

Tosser's Choice

Go to third base. Have one partner stay at home plate while a second player goes to first and acts as first baseman.

Action begins as you take your normal position off the bag. The player at home, tosser, mixes throwing the ball down the line, short hoppers, high pop flies, or slow rollers. You must concentrate and be ready to go in any direction immediately. Switch positions after fielding and throwing six balls.

Bunt Play

Repeat the procedure for "Tosser's Choice" with one exception: Send a fourth player to the mound.

Action begins when the tosser rolls a "bunt" onto the infield and calls out the situation. For example, after releasing the ball the tosser yells "runner on first." You charge, field, and throw to first (unless the coach prefers you to stay close to the bag and have the pitcher field).

Have the tosser mix hollering "runner on first," "runners on first and second," and "runner on second," or any other situation requiring fast thinking and quick reflexes. Switch positions after fielding and throwing six balls.

TIPS AND SUGGESTIONS FOR THE THIRD BASEMAN

Here are several guidelines to help your third baseman strengthen her position:

1. Tag the runner with the back of your glove. Make the tag quickly. Then pull your hand back before the runner has time to kick the ball out of your hands.
2. Listen to your catcher when lining up a throw from the outfield (runner on second, base hit to left). She will either yell "Cut," or say nothing, depending on the throw's chance of getting the runner at home.
3. Straddle the bag when tagging out a runner. Concentrate on catching the ball before applying the tag.
4. Play fairly close to the bag. Remember, it is easier to go left than to your right.
5. Charge hard off the base. You must get a good jump, especially on slow bouncers and bunts.
6. Get rid of the ball quickly.
7. Study the hitter and play your position accordingly. For example, you would stay close to the bag for a right-handed pull hitter.
8. Get together with fellow infielders. Decide ahead of time what to do in bunting situations, how to play various hitters, and when to play deep or shallow.

POINTS TO REMEMBER

What does it take to play third base? An aggressive, heads-up athlete who isn't afraid to field hard smashes down the line, throw off-balance, or get dirty tagging out sliding runners. It requires quick reflexes, fast heads, and the ability to charge forward without delay.

Undoubtedly, a third baseman must be a good fielder with a strong arm. She should be able to concentrate, think fast, and make the right move at the right time.

7. *Drills, Activities, and Games for Infielders*

THIS SECTION WILL PROVIDE you, the coach, with activities to give your infielders. Selection, of course, will depend on team need, space availability, and the number of players you wish to include.

We will cover the following areas in this chapter:

1. How to get the most out of infield practice
2. Fielding activities and games for small groups
3. Fast-action team infield drills
4. Indoor drills and activities during inclement weather
5. Points to remember

HOW TO GET THE MOST OUT OF INFIELD PRACTICE

There are five key ingredients to making infield practice go. They are: (1) Keeping the working group small; (2) Getting everybody in the group involved; (3) Keeping activities short and moving briskly; (4) Changing activities often, and; (5) Matching activities to meet the needs of the group.

Let's take a closer look at each one.

1. *Keeping the working group small.* Working with eight players or less allows you to cover more ground in a shorter period of time. If

you have more than eight infielders, you can divide them into two equal groups. While you work with one group, the other can practice bunting, sliding, or any skill you wish to develop. Groups can take turns trading off.

2. *Getting everybody in the group involved.* The secret of sustaining player interest is to give every athlete something to do. In short, you must keep them busy. Each activity should include plenty of running, fielding, and throwing. In order for players to try hard, they should see immediate results and know why they are performing certain drills and activities.

3. *Keeping activities short and moving briskly.* A fast-paced drill which lasts twenty minutes or less brings satisfactory results. Athletes won't become fatigued or bored if they stay on the move. Here's a good technique: When player interest reaches its peak, stop the activity and immediately switch to something else. Stay flexible. Have two or three alternate activities ready to go.

4. *Changing activities often.* You will want to keep the best four or five drills on hand to use when athletes ask for them. However, avoid using your best drill too often or athletes will lose interest and give a half-hearted effort.

When you organize practice sessions, make room for fresh ideas. Look for new or innovative ways to breathe life into standard drills and activities. Remain flexible enough to change activities at a moment's notice. Your athletes will develop quick-thinking skills if you frequently change or mix activities. Moving rapidly from one activity to another keeps athletes alert, active, and interested.

5. *Matching activities to meet the needs of the group.* How well athletes perform in games and practice sessions gives a clear idea of their overall playing ability and team strength. If, for instance, the infield averages six errors per game through the first three games, concentration in practice should be on fielding and throwing. Trying to do too much too soon only leads to confusion.

FIELDING ACTIVITIES AND GAMES
FOR SMALL GROUPS

These activities are designed for infielders, four to six athletes per group. They stress fundamental softball skills, including objectives, procedures, and additional comments as needed.

When athletes learn the activities, send two or three groups to various areas on the field. Combine drills into circuit stations. For example, divide athletes into groups and give them fifteen to twenty minutes per drill before moving them to the next station. Drill length, as previously mentioned, varies with equipment and facility availability, practice time, and player need.

FOUR-PLAYER DRILLS

Round Up

Objective: To practice making accurate throws.

Procedure: Four infielders go to an open area in the field. They bring four softballs, four rubber bases, and gloves with them.

Athletes form a square, each girl staying about 45 feet apart. The square should look like this: Player 1, southwest corner; Player 2, northwest corner; Player 3, northeast corner; Player 4, southeast corner. Each athlete places a ball 20 to 30 feet directly in front of her base toward the center of the square. All balls form a small square within the larger square.

Action begins when Player 1 charges, fields her placed ball, and throws it to Player 2. Player 2 throws the ball to Player 3, Player 3 relays the ball to Player 4, Player 4 returns the ball to Player 1, and Player 1 replaces the ball. Each athlete, in turn, fields and throws her placed ball. Play continues for three rounds, each player fields and throws her placed ball three times. Athletes reverse procedure and continue for three additional rounds; e.g., Player 2 fields and throws to Player 4, Player 4 relays to Player 3, and so on.

Note: Infielders work on fielding stationary balls and throwing from their left and right side. Athletes should play their regular positions—that is, Player 2, third baseman/shortstop; Player 3, second baseman/shortstop; Player 4, first baseman; Player 1, catcher.

Cross Toss

Objective: To practice fielding ground balls and making accurate throws.

Procedure: The procedure is the same as "*Round Up*" except players field and throw a moving ball.

Round One begins when Player 1 flips a ground ball to Player 3. Player 3 charges, fields, and throws the ball to Player 2. Player 2 throws to Player 4, Player 4 throws to Player 1, and Player 1 tosses the ball to Player 2. Action continues when Player 2 throws a ground ball to Player 4, and so forth.

The cycle continues according to the following scheme:

Second Round: 2 to 4 to 3 to 1 to 2 to 3

Third Round: 3 to 1 to 4 to 2 to 3 to 4

Fourth Round: 4 to 2 to 1 to 3 to 4 to 1

Note: Players must stay alert and concentrate on making accurate throws. Once organized this activity is very impressive to watch.

Fetch

Objective: To practice running, fielding, and throwing.

Procedure: Four athletes, carrying gloves, go to an open area in the outfield.

Players 1 and 2 stand about 80 to 100 (optional) feet apart, facing each other. Players 3 and 4, standing side-by-side, stay about 100 feet to the right and between Players 1 and 2.

Player 1, holding a ball, yells "Go." Player 3 runs at an angle toward Player 2. Player 1 tosses a fly ball, pop fly, line drive, or ground ball ahead of Player 3. Player 3 fields and tosses the ball to Player 4, then returns. Player 4 throws the ball to Player 2. Player 2 tosses it to Player 1. Player 4 becomes the fielder and action resumes.

Players 3 and 4 field the ball three times before moving to the left side of Players 1 and 2. They field three more balls apiece. Everybody rotates clockwise—Player 1 becomes 2, Player 2 becomes 3, and so on. Each athlete fields three balls from the left side and right side of Players 1 and 2.

FIVE-PLAYER DRILLS

T Sprint

Objective: To practice running, fielding, and throwing.

Procedure: Five players bring their gloves and a softball to an open area in the field. They make a letter T in the manner described below.

Players 1, 2, and 4 make a vertical line, staying approximately 50 feet apart. Players 3 and 5 complete the T by forming a horizontal line. Player 3 stays about 50 feet to the left of Player 4; Player 5 stands about 50 feet to the right of Player 4.

$$3 \quad 4 \quad 5$$
$$2 \text{ (tosser)}$$
$$1 \text{ (fielder)}$$

Player 2 (tosser) starts action by rolling a ball to the left of Player 1 (fielder). Player 1 charges, fields, and throws the ball across field to Player 5. Player 1 returns to her starting position. Player 5 tosses the ball back to Player 2. Player 2 rolls the ball to the right of Player 1. Player 1 charges, fields, and throws the ball across field to Player 3. Player 1 returns to her starting position. Player 3 tosses the ball back to Player 2. When Player 2 yells "Go," Player 1 sprints toward Player 4, passes her, and continues to run straight ahead. Player 2 throws a long fly ball to Player 1. Player 2 moves to the spot vacated by Player 1; Player 4 drops into the spot vacated by Player 2. Player 1 fields and throws the ball to Player 2. Player 4, cut-off man, stops off-target throws. Player 2 directs action. She yells "cut" for wild throws.

After Player 1 fields three balls, players rotate to the next number; i.e., Player 1 becomes 2, Player 2 becomes 3, and so forth.

Note: This drill provides plenty of exercise for each athlete. After two or three rounds, step up the pace by using two balls; i.e., Player 2 throws two balls, seconds apart. Player 2 can mix her tosses—low grounders, high choppers, single bouncers, high-fly balls, and so on.

Hustle

Objective: To practice fielding and throwing.

Procedure: Five players bring their gloves, a rubber base, and three balls to an open area in the field. The rubber base marks the starting line. Place three balls in a straight line, 30 feet apart, and vertical with the rubber base. Player 1, pick-up man, stands on the starting line facing the three balls. Player 2, back-up man, remains behind the starting line. Player 4 stands about 120 feet away from Player 1 and in line with the three balls. Player 3 stays about 50 feet to the left of Player 4; Player 5 remains approximately 50 feet to the right of Player 4.

Action begins when Player 2 yells "Go." Player 1 runs to the first ball, fields, and throws it to Player 3. She fields and throws the second ball to Player 4. Finally, she fields and throws the third ball to Player 5. Players 3, 4, and 5, in turn, toss the ball back to Player 1— ground ball or fly ball. Player 1 fields each ball and returns it to Player 2. Player 2 replaces the balls. Athletes rotate to the next number; i.e., Player 1 becomes 2, Player 2 becomes 3, and so on.

Note: "Hustle" is an excellent drill for every player, especially pitchers, any time during the season. It involves running, bending, stretching, and throwing. Players 3, 4, and 5 should make Player 1 work hard by throwing the ball beyond her reach or far to one side.

SIX-PLAYER DRILLS

Fielder in the Ring

Objective: To practice fielding and throwing.

Procedure: Six players bring their gloves and a ball to an open area in the field. They form a circle according to Figure 7.1. The fielder, Player 6, stands in the middle of the ring.

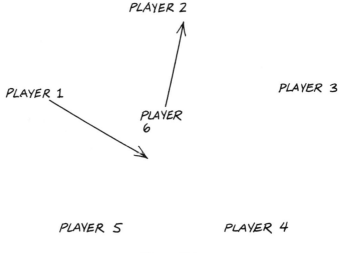

Figure 7.1

Action begins when Player 1 tosses a ball—hard grounder, high bouncer, or low line drive—to the left or right of Player 6. Player 6 fields and makes a return throw to Player 2. Athletes standing behind the fielder recover missed balls. If Player 6 fumbles the ball, athletes move up a number and continue play; i.e., Player 6 becomes Player 1, Player 2, becomes Player 3, and so forth. Player 5 replaces Player 6 in the ring.

Have athletes field and throw for about five minutes before playing for points. Scoring is as follows:

1 point—Ball fielded cleanly

1 point—Accurate throw

Suggestion: Have athletes give a stationary chest-high target with their gloves. If the fielder can hit the target without an athlete moving her glove, award two points. The fielder loses all points if she makes a fielding or throwing error. The athlete with the most points after 20 minutes of action wins.

Note: The tosser controls the pace of the drill. She must adjust her tosses to challenge the fielder and, at the same time, not push her beyond her ability.

Stoop

Objective: To practice running, fielding, and throwing.

Procedure: Six players bring four rubber bases, gloves, and six balls to an open area in the field. They make a diamond, bases about 46 feet apart.

Athletes divide into two teams, three players per team. Team A comes to home plate; Team B, defense, sends players to first base, second base, and third base. Team B places the balls on the field in this manner: two, one foot apart, 25 or 30 feet down the first base line; two, one foot apart, 25 or 30 feet down the third base line; and two, one foot apart, approximately 25 or 30 feet in front of home plate.

Rules for "*Stoop*":

- Each Team A player fields and throws all six balls, one at a time, to each infielder in succession.
- Each Team A player fields and throws balls lying along the third base line to the first baseman, balls lying along the first base line to the third baseman, and balls resting in front of home plate to the second baseman.
- After player fields and throws all six balls, she runs the bases.
- Team B athletes replace all balls.

- After each player on Team A completes two rounds, sides change. Time dictates the number of rounds played.

- Award one point for clean pickups and accurate throws. The team earning the most points wins.

Note: Go over base-running techniques prior to the drill. Show athletes how to round bases by cutting to the inside corner of the bag. Remind players to concentrate on making accurate throws.

FAST-ACTION INFIELD DRILLS

These next four activities are popular among infielders because they require excellent fielding and throwing to be successful. The best time to use these drills is at the end of practice.

Four Score

Objective: To practice fielding and throwing.

Procedure: Infielders form two groups. Group A, fielders, line up near shortstop. Group B, runners, come to home plate.

Action begins when the coach hits four balls, one at a time, to the left, to the right, or directly at the first fielder in line. The athlete, assuming a low fielding position, must be ready for anything hit her way.

As soon as the coach hits a ball to the fielder, a runner breaks for first base. She continues running the bases until she reaches home plate. A back-up player (runner waiting her turn) catches the throws from the fielder.

Award points in the following manner:

1 point —Player fields cleanly and makes a good throw to the back-up person.

2 points—The last throw beats the runner to home plate.

If the fielder makes an error, she loses all of her points. The coach judges every play.

After an athlete fields and throws four times, she goes to home plate. After the runner circles the bases, she goes to shortstop. The activity consists of two rounds or eight chances to field and throw. An athlete, playing two rounds, can score up to ten points.

Note: Make sure runners wear protective equipment. Do not let runners slide into home plate. Advise the back-up person to stay behind home plate and not to attempt to tag out the runner.

Strike Three

Objective: To concentrate on making accurate throws to home plate.

Procedure: Infielders, including catcher, take their positions.

Action begins when the coach hits a ground ball to the third baseman. The third baseman fields and throws to the catcher. The throw must enter the strike zone or be easy enough for the catcher to handle with no difficulty. Each athlete, in turn, fields and throws home. If a player throws off-target, the drill starts over. For example, if the second baseman throws wild, then the coach hits a ball to the third baseman again.

Continue play until athletes can complete two rounds of action without error. This is a good warm-up drill prior to regular infield practice.

Note: Athletes bear down since peer pressure encourages concentration. Ask your catcher to give a clear target over home plate.

One Step Ahead

Objective: To stress getting rid of the ball quickly and throwing accurately.

Procedure: Infielders, excluding pitchers, take their positions. Runners line up at home plate. They go full speed around the bases, one at a time.

Action begins when the coach hits a ball to an infielder, for example, the third baseman. A runner heads for first and continues to round the bases. The infielder throws the ball to first base. From there it is relayed around the infield twice. The third baseman does not touch the ball the second time around. The athlete fielding the ball automatically drops out of the action when the ball goes around a second time. If the ball isn't dropped, bobbled, or wildly thrown, it will reach the catcher one step ahead of the average runner. Every infielder receives two chances to field the ball.

Note: Pitchers make excellent baserunners. Anytime a runner beats the ball around the infield, make all infielders do five push-ups apiece. They'll work harder.

Champ or Chump

Objective: To provide a fast-paced, interesting infield drill.

Procedure: All infielders, excluding catchers, line up in a semi-circle between second and third base. The coach stands between the pitcher's mound and the third baseline. A pick-up person (catcher) stands to the coach's right. The champ is a player who performs flawlessly during the drill. The idea is to become the champ by playing errorless ball. Clean fielding and throwing are necessary for success in this drill.

The rules are as follows:

1. Infielders must field and throw accurately to the pick-up player. A poorly thrown ball results in the infielder's becoming chump.

2. The coach decides who will become champ and chump before the drill begins. The champ may be the athlete who won this title in a previous drill.

3. Action begins when the coach hits balls easily, then progressively livens up the drill by adding speed to ground balls. An infielder must play any type of ball hit into her area.

4. The infielder cannot pretend to field the ball or crowd another player. A violation of this rule results in the athlete becoming the chump.

5. If the ball is mishandled or thrown wild to the pick-up player, the athlete runs over to second base, touches the bag with her foot, sprints into left field, and changes places with the chump.

6. Players move one position at a time from right or left (from the second toward third base) only when errors are made.

7. The chump acts as backup for any balls hit through the legs or over the heads of the infielders. She can come back to the fielding zone when errors are committed. The chump takes her place at third base at the end of the line (position nearest second base.)

8. The champ can only be dethroned when she makes an error. Then she becomes the chump. The champ is subject to harder hit balls because her position is so close to the coach. Since she is champ, her right to the title is continually challenged.

9. Sharply hit balls or line drives deemed base hits are not recognized as errors. The coach serves as the judge.

Note: The values obtained from this drill are threefold: (a) The coach controls the speed and type of ball he or she wishes to hit; (b) The infielders quickly realize that success comes only through sound use of fielding techniques; and (c) This drill motivates athletes because it provides the incentive for becoming *The Champ.*

INDOOR DRILLS AND ACTIVITIES DURING INCLEMENT WEATHER

Rain or cold may cut practice time or drive your team indoors. The problem many coaches face during inclement weather is what team—track, soccer, softball, baseball, etc.—will be able to use the gym. It's hard to schedule the gym in advance since no one knows for sure when poor weather conditions will arrive.

When two or three teams share the gym, you may only be able to work inside with a small group of athletes. If you elect to bring infielders into the gym, try the following activities:

Wall Rebound

Objective: To sharpen fielding reflexes.

Procedure: Divide players into two groups, six to eight per group. Send each group to a different area of the gym. Give each group a soft rubber ball.

Separate each group into two teams, A and B. Have players line up facing the gym wall. Keep teams several feet apart, about 30 feet from the gym wall.

Action begins when Player A tosses the ball at eye level against the gym wall; Player B fields the rebound. Player B receives points for accurate fielding according to the following point system:

Line Drive	1 point—Player must catch the ball in flight.
Single Bounce	1 point—Player traps or fields the ball after it hits the floor in front of her.
Grounder	½ point—Player fields the ball after it strikes the ground two or more times.

If the fielder makes an error any time during the game, she loses all points and must start over again. If a player makes a bad throw which causes the ball to deflect to one side or bounce high in the air, Player B receives a one-half point bonus. She also receives another turn. Player A loses one-half point from her total score.

Note: Check the wall surface for anything that may cause deflection. Lay a strip of tape, eye level across the wall. This helps athletes make accurate throws.

After Player A throws the ball, she must not interfere with Player B. If any player interferes with Player B, Player B receives one point, plus another turn. The guilty athlete loses one point from her total score. After throwing the ball, Player A goes to the end of Line A. The first athlete to earn ten points wins.

Act Fast

Objective: To sharpen fielding reflexes.

Procedure: Athletes follow the same procedure suggested
in " *Wall Rebound*" with these additions:

Player B turns back to wall. When Player A throws the ball against the wall and hollers "field," Player B quickly turns, locates the ball, and fields the rebound.

Player A throws the ball against the gym floor approximately one to two feet in front of the wall. She adjusts her tosses according to the type of rebound desired. For instance, if she wants a high, lofty fly ball, she throws the ball hard against the floor. If she wants a soft bouncer or fly ball, she throws the ball easily against the floor.

Combine "*Wall Rebound*" and "*Act Fast.*" Athletes must stay alert and be ready to move quickly in any direction.

Line 'Em Up

Objective: To practice fielding and throwing.

Procedure: Players form two lines, A and B, about 40 feet
apart. The coach stands about three feet from
the gym wall and faces both teams. The
players stay from 50 to 60 feet away, facing
the coach.

Action begins when the coach throws a soft rubber ball between the first players in each line. When the ball passes the players, the coach calls out "A" or "B."

Athletes wait in a fielding position. If the coach hollers "A," Player A pivots, turns, and runs after the ball. Player B lines up between the coach and Player A. She becomes the relay person. Player A fields and throws the ball to Player B. She concentrates on throwing the ball shoulder-high to the glove side. Player B relays the ball to the coach.

Player A then sprints toward Player B. When she reaches Player B, Player B runs to the area vacated by Player A. The coach throws a fast bouncer or long fly ball to Player B. Player B returns a chest-high throw to the coach. Player A now becomes a cut-off person. Player A goes to the end of line B; Player B goes to the end of Line A.

Award points in the following manner:

- 2 points—Player A makes an exceptional catch of a fly ball or line drive.
- 1 point —Shoulder-high throws on the relay person's glove side.
- 1 point —Off-target throws or misplayed balls.
- 2 points—Players who fail to hustle.

The first athlete earning ten points wins.

Streak

Objective: To practice fielding while moving quickly straight ahead.

Procedure: Divide athletes into two groups. Send each group to a different area of the gym. Players stand facing the gym wall, approximately 50 feet away. The coach (or designated player) stands between the players and gym wall, about 10 or 15 feet to the left or right. A strip of tape is placed on the gym wall, six to eight feet above the floor.

Action begins when the coach or designated player yells "Go." The first player in line sprints toward the wall. When she gets within 30 feet of the wall, the coach throws a soft rubber ball slightly above the taped zone. The athlete fields the rebound and makes a return throw to the coach.

The rebound, a difficult ball to handle, bounces immediately in front of the fielder. Each athlete receives three chances to field and throw. A competitive point system can be set up as follows:

1 point—For clean block; i.e., athlete keeps body in front of ball and fields it cleanly.

½ point—Player blocks ball, but bobbles it. However, she keeps the ball in front of her.

0 point—Ball rolls between fielder's legs, goes to one side, or the fielder catches it on the fly.

The first athlete earning six points wins. *Note:* Two things determine the success of the drill: Player distance from the wall and tape height. Make the proper adjustments by throwing a ball against the wall prior to the drill. Athletes learn to keep their bodies in direct line with the ball. Players realize the importance of watching the ball all the way into their gloves during a game. If a ball bounces off a player's chest and falls in front of her, she still has a good chance to throw out the runner.

Underhand Roll and Go

Objective: To keep athletes moving about.

Procedure: Divide the players into two equal groups, A and B. Each group splits into two equal teams. The two teams in each group separate and form a line 90 to 100 feet apart, facing one another. Groups A and B stay about 40 feet apart.

Action begins when the coach hollers "Go." The first player in each line rolls a soft rubber ball underhand to the first player in line facing her. After tossing underhand, the player races to the end of the opposite line. The receiving player fields the ball, throws it to the next person in the opposite line, then sprints to the end of that line. The athlete receiving the ball rolls underhand to the next player in the opposite line, and so on.

Action continues for two rounds (optional). Each player receives two chances to toss and field the ball. Erring players recover misplayed balls. Teammates are not allowed to assist. Assisting player pays by running laps or doing extra push-ups.

Players compete against each other while conditioning their bodies for season play. Athletes stay busy; there is little time for horseplay.

POINTS TO REMEMBER

In many cases, how well an athlete performs during practice depends on her readiness to play and her attitude regarding self-improvement.

Athletes grow stale from doing the same thing every day in practice. These dull, slow-moving sessions dampen their desire to excel. A smart coach knows that flexibility in planning activities is the secret to motivating athletes and encouraging them to improve.

The best practice sessions seem to be those which include fast-moving activities for small groups. Twenty-minute drills that keep athletes hustling and competing against each other sustain player interest.

During inclement weather you might have to scratch and claw for a tiny corner of the gym. Grab what you can and take your athletes inside. A brief session with a handful of players keeps spirits alive and helps infielders stay in tune.

8. Outfield

SOME ATHLETES BALK at playing the outfield because they say action is slow and the coach may use the outfield as a dumping ground by putting a poor-fielding, slow-moving player in right field, for example.

It's true the outfielder may field fewer balls than an infielder, but a smart coach realizes that a team's success hinges on the heads-up play of every athlete at every position.

As a coach, you know that playing the outfield requires an athlete to stay mentally alert and physically fit at all times. Therefore, you must do everything possible to develop a strong outfield. The question is: How?

PREPARING THE OUTFIELDER FOR COMPETITION

First of all, you need athletes who have fair to good speed, strong arms, and excellent fielding ability. Once you decide which athletes will play the outfield, gather them together and stress those activities necessary for successful team play. For example:

- How to warm up properly
- How to employ a cross-seam grip and make accurate overhand throws
- How to hit the cut-off player with a strong, hard throw
- How to properly field ground balls, line drives, and fly balls
- How to improve fielding and throwing skills through gamelike activities and drills

Now let's see how these activities fit into the overall practice plan.

WARM-UP EXERCISES FOR OUTFIELDERS

It is especially important for an outfielder to warm up properly and prepare her arm for making long, hard throws. Throwing the ball during pregame infield/outfield will not stretch the muscles of the throwing arm sufficiently to offset the risk of injury.

You can make sure your outfielders stretch their throwing arm muscles by asking them to do the following four exercises (right-handed player). These simple activities take less than five minutes to complete.

Exercise One:
Double-Arm Hang

Grab an overhanging bar with both hands. Make sure your feet do not touch the ground. Gradually relax allowing your arms and hands to support your body weight. Hang from 10 to 15 seconds. Release grip. Take a 30-second rest.

Exercise Two:
Single-Arm Hang

Repeat procedure for "Double Arm Hang." After grabbing the bar with both hands, release the grip of your left hand. Support body weight with your right arm only. Hang from 10 to 15 seconds. Release grip. Take a 30-second rest.

Exercise Three:
Upper-Arm Pull

Stand erect with your feet shoulder-width apart. Bend forward at the waist, place fingers of right hand, palm up, under sole of right foot. Lock your elbow and keep your arm straight. Now slowly pull upward as you straighten your back. Pull steadily from 10 to 15 seconds. Release grip. Take a 30-second rest.

Exercise Four:
Single-Arm/Leg Touch

Lie flat on your back. Place your left arm alongside your body. Stretch out your right arm and leg by extending them outward. Now touch your right hand to your right toe holding both arm and leg straight. Hold position for three to five seconds. Release and return to rest position. Repeat 10 to 15 times.

Allow outfielders to work on their own or hold group warm-up/ exercise prior to throwing. Players may prefer to hang from backstop wire. Warn them about protruding pieces of sharp metal.

TEACHING THE PROPER THROWING GRIP

A comfortable, firm grip allows outfielders to pinpoint throwing accuracy. Most coaches teach their outfielders to throw with a two-or three-fingered grip on the ball.

If you want your outfielders to use a two-fingered cross-seam grip, have them:

- Place first and second fingers across the seams of the ball. Keep fingers about one-half to three-fourths of an inch apart. Let the ball rest over the thumb.

- Make sure the ball stays forward, away from the palm. A cross-seam grip allows the ball to spin backward and follow a straight path.

- For proper placement and balance, turn throwing hand palm up. Place the ball on the first two fingers of throwing hand. Use third finger to steady the ball. Adjust the ball until it feels comfortable. Now press thumb firmly against the ball.

- Bring throwing arm high overhead. Hold onto ball and snap arm forward several times simulating a throwing motion. Now check grip. This will be the natural grip and should bring pleasing results.

If you prefer the three-fingered cross-seam grip, have your players do this:

- Place first, second, and third fingers across the seams of the ball. Keep them about one-quarter to one inch apart. Let the ball rest over the thumb. The fourth finger helps the thumb support the ball.

It doesn't matter which grip your players use as long as they can control the ball and make accurate throws. Players with small hands might do better using a three-fingered grip.

Remind players not to watch their fingers grip the ball before they throw it. This, of course, wastes time and momentarily takes their minds off the play.

If you have an outfielder who watches her fingers grip the ball, tell her to practice this activity:

Find a partner. Bring gloves and five balls with you to an open space. Set the balls in a straight, east-west line approximately three feet apart. Stand 15 to 20 feet behind and to the left of the first ball (the nearest ball). Have your partner stand facing you about 60 feet away.

Take your fielding position. When your partner yells "Go," run to Ball 1 (the nearest ball), pick it up with your bare hand and make a chest-high, glove-side throw to your partner. Concentrate on finding a comfortable grip without looking at the ball. If your hand is small, pick up the ball with your bare hand and glove. Hold the ball next to your glove while you adjust the grip.

After you field and throw each ball, check with your partner. Make sure your ball spins properly and doesn't sail or tail away. Now have your partner repeat the procedure.

The motion of changing the ball from the glove to the hand must be quick and sure. To make sure your players get a proper grip on the ball, check to see that their hands go in and take the ball out of the glove. The ball must never be flipped out of the glove into the hand.

SHOWING OUTFIELDERS
HOW TO MAKE ACCURATE THROWS

Remind outfielders that the grip is only one small part of the throwing picture. The arm and body motion must work together in a smooth manner to keep the ball on target.

Pass along the following ten throwing tips to your athletes (right-handed thrower):

- Hold the ball with a cross-seam grip. Do not grip the ball too tightly.
- Keep your eyes fixed on the target.
- As you begin to throw, point your front or pivot foot and left shoulder toward the target.
- Draw arm back keeping elbow even with shoulder. Be careful not to let arm drop.
- Shift hips and shoulders to throwing-side of body. Swing body weight over front foot.
- Lift and extend left foot toward target. Reach back with throwing arm. Hold left arm (glove hand) out in front for balance.
- Keep weight on right foot as left foot lifts off ground to start the step forward.

- Shift body weight from pivot foot to the left leg. Rotate shoulder and hips forward so that body faces target. Bring right arm directly over the top; weight transfers to left foot.
- Release the ball with a complete follow-through motion. The wrist snaps in a downward motion on the follow-through.
- Concentrate on bending at the waist and snapping the wrist. To emphasize the waist bend, reach down with your throwing hand and touch the grass. Your hips will rotate 180 degrees with your right foot taking a step forward.

The crowhop is a technique your athletes can use when they need to make long throws. It allows them to get more momentum (using their bodies) behind the throw in order to put more power on the throw. This motion takes more time to complete because of the extra step involved.

Give these instructions to your players: After you catch the ball, step with your left foot, hop on the right foot, step with the left foot again, and throw. Follow through with your right foot (Figure 8.1).

Figure 8.1a

Figure 8.1b

Figure 8.1c

Tell athletes that once their arm muscles loosen, they can begin throwing. The throwing routine, like the series of warm-up exercises, should follow an established pattern designed to prepare athletes for practice or game conditions.

Here is a 15- to 20-minute, three-part overhand throwing drill you can include in your practices. Give these instructions:

Part One:
Back-Up Catch (5 Minutes)

Pair off. Begin by throwing easy overhand tosses to your partner. Concentrate on throwing the ball chest-high and to the glove side. Try to hit the pocket of your partner's glove.

After making eight to ten throws, take three steps backward. After eight to ten more throws, have your partner step back three paces. Alternate backing up and throwing for five minutes. Then switch to Part Two.

Part Two:
Left-Right (5 Minutes)

Toss a fly ball or ground ball to the left side of your partner. After releasing the ball, break to your left, run about twenty feet, and stop. Hold your glove chest-high and have your partner make an overhand throw. Return the ball by making an overhand throw to your partner's glove side.

Repeat the procedure. This time have your partner toss the ball to your right side before she breaks to her right. Alternate throwing and fielding for five minutes. Then switch to Part Three.

Part Three:
One-Hop (5 Minutes)

Stand about 80 to 100 feet apart. Take turns making overhand, one-hop throws with a complete follow-through motion. Try to keep all bounces waist-high and in front of your partner. Adjust your throwing speed and distance accordingly. Alternate throwing and fielding for five minutes.

Stress to your athletes the importance of warming up properly. Keep player spirit high by showing constant enthusiasm and praising successful throws.

Pass along the following points:

- Throw with a purpose. Try to hit your target with each overhand toss.

- Make these drills challenging by competing against your partner. You can do this by awarding one point for each throw on target. The player with the most points wins.

FOUR FAST-MOVING PARTNER THROWING DRILLS

Now let's speed things up. The following four drills will test the ability of your players to make accurate overhand throws. Give your athletes these instructions:

Side Ball

Bring your partner, gloves, and four balls to an open field. Stand about 60 feet away from your partner. When you are ready, have your partner throw you the ball. Catch it and give it a short toss to one side. Let the ball stop rolling. Then charge the ball, pick it up, and throw to your partner. Try to hit her glove side about chest high. Have her repeat the procedure. Continue play for about ten minutes, tossing the ball from side-to-side.

Speed Ball

Stand about 60 feet away from your partner. Make a diamond pattern out of four balls. When your partner says "Go," run to a ball, pick it up, and throw to your partner. Then pick up and throw the rest of the balls as fast as you can. You'll find that it's very hard to make good throws when you are in a hurry. However, you can still throw accurately if you keep your eyes on the target. Now switch and let your partner field and throw. For added interest, include this rule: If a player makes a wild throw, she must run after the ball. Play "Speed Ball" until each player can make twelve good tosses in a row.

Zigzag

Place four balls in a zigzag fashion between you and your partner. Keep balls about ten feet apart. Stand about 90 feet away from your partner. When your partner yells "Go," run to Ball 1 (nearest ball), pick it up, and make a single-bounce throw to your partner. Do the same for Ball 2. When you field Ball 3 and Ball 4, make a chest-high, glove-side throw to your partner. Replace each ball and let your partner field and throw.

Quick Shift

Place two balls about 20 to 25 feet apart. Stand between the two balls and stay about 60 feet away from your partner. On the command "Go," break to your left, field Ball 1, and make an overhand throw to your partner. Have your partner toss a bouncing ball to your right. Field the ball and make an overhand return throw. Return to the starting point. On the command "Go," repeat the same procedure. This time break to the right. Repeat the drill five times before switching with your partner.

Coaching Tips:

- Keep throwing drills short (15–20 minutes), fast-moving and challenging. Throwing for throwing's sake slows down practice and quickly bores the players.
- Have players warm up properly before attempting to throw hard. Make sure they wear a sweater or jacket on cold, windy days.
- If a player has trouble following through, have her try this: Place a small object—coin, washer, or rock—out in front of her body. After she releases the ball, have her pick up the object with her throwing arm. This will help bring her arm over and down after the ball leaves her hand.

GROUP COMPETITIVE THROWING DRILLS

Most coaches agree that hitting the relay or cut-off player with an accurate throw is the most important play an outfielder can make.

One way to make certain that your outfielders get adequate throwing practice to develop accuracy is to set up the shovel/net target. This is a device which resembles both a tool for digging clams and a fish net (Figure 8.2). The target serves one purpose: to improve throwing accuracy.

In order to build a shovel/net target, simply tape the handle of a fish net to the handle of a shovel. Use a net with a wide opening, and make certain the net is strong enough to withstand the force of a thrown ball.

When the target is ready, drive the spade end of the shovel into the ground with your foot. Keep the shovel in an upright position. The net opening should be about five feet above the ground.

Stand facing the target and toss several balls into the net. Wind up and throw hard. Let the ball smack into the net. If everything checks out, then the target is ready to be set up for three competitive drills which will test the throwing arms of your outfielders.

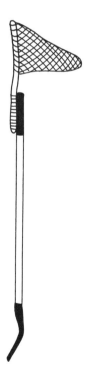

Figure 8.2

Still Ball

Have outfielders (3–8) bring the shovel/net target and three balls to an open area. Have players form a line, staying about five feet apart (Figure 8.3). A back-up player (outfielder) stands about 30 or 40 feet directly behind the target. Her job is to field the thrown balls. The "catcher" (outfielder) stands either to the left or to the right, and somewhere between the outfielders in line and the back-up player. *Note:* You can take part in these drills by acting as the "catcher."

Place the target approximately 90 feet (optional) from the outfielders. Three balls are set, as shown in Figure 8.3. Action begins when the "catcher" calls "Go." Player 1, the first athlete in line, sprints to Ball 1, picks it up, and executes an overhand throw to the target. The athlete concentrates on tossing the ball into the net. After throwing the ball, Player 1 runs to Ball 2, picks it up, and throws at the target. Player 1 repeats the procedure until she has thrown all three balls and returns to the end of the line.

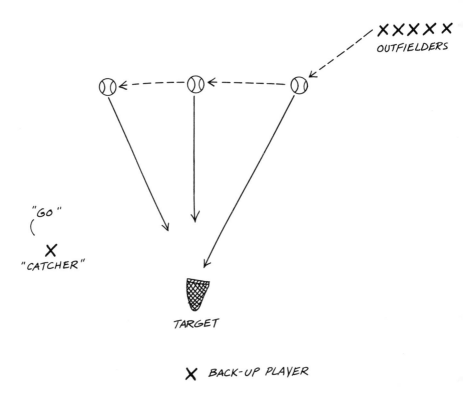

Figure 8.3

The back-up player fields and throws each ball to the "catcher." After Player 1 completes the drill, the "catcher" returns each ball to it original position.

After Player 1 goes to the line and the "catcher" returns the balls, Player 2 takes off when the "catcher" calls "Go." Each player runs the circuit four times and makes a total of twelve throws. Players take turns acting as backup.

Spice up the drill by awarding points for accurate throws. Allow points for hitting the shovel handle, net handle, or rim, or for throwing the ball into the net. Use the following scoring system: 1. A player earns points only if the ball hits the shovel handle or net while in flight; that is, the ball cannot bounce first before making contact; 2. A player earns one point if a throw hits the shovel handle; 3. A player earns two points if a throw hits the fishing net; either handle, rim, or strings; 4. A player earns five points if a throw lands inside the net. The back-up player acts as a judge and awards points accordingly. The player earning the most points after four rounds (twelve throws) wins.

Flip and Toss

The purpose of the second drill is to practice fielding and executing accurate overhand throws. The equipment needed is a shovel/net target and two balls. The procedure is identical to "Still Ball," with the following changes:

The "catcher" holds two balls. On the command "Go," Player 1 sprints toward the "catcher." The "catcher" flips Ball 1 to the left of Player 1. Player 1 fields and throws overhand to the target (Figure 8.4).

After throwing the ball, Player 1 breaks to her right. The "catcher" flips the second ball 20 to 30 feet in front of Player 1. Player 1 fields, throws, and returns to the line. The back-up player returns both balls to the "catcher."

After Player 1 returns to the line, the "catcher" yells "Go" and Player 2 takes off. Each player runs the circuit four times and earns points for hitting the target.

Fungo Toss

The purpose of the third drill is again to practice fielding and making accurate overhand throws. Equipment needed is the shovel/net target, fungo bat, and ball. The procedure is the same as for the first two drills, with these changes:

Players position themselves as shown in the illustration. The "catcher" calls "Go," tosses a ball into the air, and hits it in front of

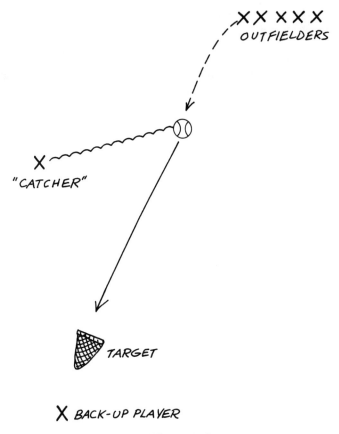

Figure 8.4

Player 1. Player 1 fields and throws overhand to the target. The "catcher" should vary the hits, mixing sharp bouncing balls with high fly balls. The back-up player returns the ball to the "catcher."

After Player 1 returns to the line, the "catcher" again gives the command and Player 2 takes off. Each player fields and throws ten to twelve times, earning points for hitting the target.

FIELDING GROUNDERS, LINE DRIVES, AND FLY BALLS

Practicing the mechanics of fielding is, of course, the main objective of building a sound defense. Through intelligent practice and a conscientious effort every outfielder can pinpoint and isolate the troublesome areas famous for causing problems. This section will discuss the mechanics of proper fielding and show you effective ways to help erring players.

Fielding Ground Balls

Here are five tips to give your players for fielding balls hit directly at them:

- Stay low. If this seems too hard, touch the ground with your glove. This will keep your body close to the ground.
- Bend at the knees and waist. Bring your body weight slightly forward over your toes.
- Extend arms out in front of body. Hold your head up. Never take your eyes off the ball.
- Get to the ball quickly. Look the ball into the glove; that is, watch it nestle deeply into the pocket.
- Come up throwing. Watch the target and make a good overhand throw.

See for yourself the value of staying low. Bring your partner, glove, and ball to an open field. Stay about 20 feet away from your partner. Rest your hands on your knees and bend forward slightly.

Have your partner toss you several fast, low-bouncing ground balls. Notice how tough it is to field when your body remains high. Now assume a low fielding position, glove touching ground. Field five or six more balls. This position makes you a better fielder because it gives you balance and allows you to see more of the ball. Remember: It's easier to come up on the ball than go down after it.

Ground Ball to the Left

Pass along these points to your players:

- Keep your eyes on the ball.
- Swing body to the left. Pivot on the balls of both feet.
- Bring your right foot across and in front of your left foot.
- Get to the ball quickly. Keep your body in front of the ball.

Ground Ball to the Right

Have your players do the following:

- Keep your eyes on the ball.
- Swing body to the right. Pivot on the balls of both feet.

- Bring your left foot across and in front of your right foot.
- Get to the ball quickly. Keep your body in front of the ball.

You can help an erring player by working one-on-one and tossing slow-moving balls to her left and to her right. Gradually increase ball speed and throwing distance as she gains confidence. When her fielding shows improvement, go to an open area and fungo balls to her.

Fielding Line Drives

Most players, especially outfielders, agree that the hardest ball to field is the one coming straight at them. Often a line drive suddenly rises or drops. Therefore, it's important to constantly remind athletes to keep their eyes on the ball at all times.

Give Outfielders These Points to Help Them Improve Their Fielding

- Extend glove hand, fingers turned upward out in front of body. Keep extended arm and glove in line with the path of the ball.
- Catch ball on glove side of body.
- After ball hits glove, bring bare hand in front of glove to keep ball from popping out.
- Make a good overhand throw.

For Line Drives Below the Waist

- Extend glove hand, fingers turned downward, out in front of body. Keep extended arm and glove in line with the path of the ball.
- Catch ball on glove side of body.
- After ball hits glove, bring bare hand in front of glove to keep ball from popping out.
- Make a good overhand throw.

For Line Drives Above the Waist

- Extend glove hand, fingers turned upward, out in front of body. Keep extended arm and glove in line with the path of the ball.
- Catch ball on glove side of body.
- After ball hits glove, bring bare hand in front of glove to keep ball from popping out.
- Make a good overhand throw.

Sinking Line Drives

Diving for the ball is a difficult technique to teach. However, if an outfielder doesn't practice diving for the ball, chances are she won't do it in a game. Therefore, take your outfielders to a grassy area devoid of obstacles such as hard ground, loose rocks, and so on. Hit shoe-top liners and "dying quails." These are balls that require an outfielder to leap forward and extend her body. This takes courage on her part.

Give outfielders the following seven tips:

- Keep your eyes on the ball.

- Get set in a ready position. Keep your feet about shoulder width apart, knees flexed, weight forward on the balls of your feet, and arms hanging loosely in front of body. Assume a ready position on each pitch and relax between pitches. Stay alert for other possible plays between pitches as well.

- Move quickly to the ball. Be off and running as the bat meets the ball in the direction of the hit. Above all, call out for the ball.

- Get your body weight under the ball. Set your feet. Keep body weight slightly over your toes.

- Hold the fingers of your glove upward. Keep arms and hands extended in front of your head.

- Try to make catch about head level. Don't turn your head to the side at the last minute. If you do, you might lose track of the ball.

- Catch the ball before you try to throw it. Then get rid of the ball quickly.

FIELDING GAMES FOR TWO, THREE, AND FOUR PLAYERS

The following competitive games allow your players to have fun while executing sound fielding and throwing fundamentals.

Give your athletes these directions:

Two-Player Games

Triangle

Go to an open area. Stand about 40 feet away and face your partner. Get into a low fielding position. Your partner begins play by tossing a ground ball to your right. Field the ball and make an overhand throw to her glove side. Return to starting point. Field two more balls—one to your left and one straight ahead.

Repeat four more times. Then switch with your partner. Each player earns one point per clean fielding play. The player with the most points after five rounds wins. A player receives no points for wild throws and misplayed or bobbled balls. *Note:* Use this scoring system for all the drills in this section.

Bombs Away

Go to an open area. Stand approximately four feet away and face your partner. Begin by tossing the ball lightly to one side of your partner, just far enough away so that she has to extend her body fully to catch the ball. *Rule:* The fielder cannot move her feet and must fall on the ground.

Mix up your tosses. Throw a few balls in front of her so she'll have to drive straight ahead to make the catch.

After throwing ten or twelve balls, switch positions; you field, your partner tosses. After the first round of play, step up the pace by allowing the fielder to move her feet. The tosser will now have to throw the ball a little farther to the sides and perhaps move back a step or two. The key to success for this drill rests with throwing accuracy. Try to make all throws between knee and waist level.

Slant

Bring three balls to an open space. Place them at a slant ten to fifteen feet apart between you and your partner. Stand about 60 feet away from your partner. Assume a low fielding position.

When your partner yells "Go," run to Ball 1, pick it up, and make an overhand throw to her glove side. Return to starting point. Get into a low fielding position. On "Go," charge Ball 2, field, and throw. Repeat same procedure for Ball 3.

Repeat four more times. Then switch with your partner. The player with the most points after five rounds wins.

Alternate games. Play "Triangle" for five rounds, then switch to "Slant." Again, to change the pace, play "Bombs Away" in combination with the other two drills.

Have players change activities often. Keep things moving with plenty of variety.

Three-Player Game

Corners

Go to an open area. Players stay about 60 feet apart (Figure 8.5). Player 1 stands between Ball 1 and Ball 2. Keep the balls at least 90 feet apart.

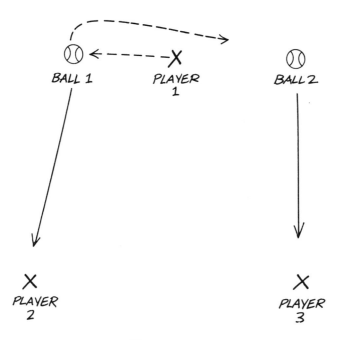

Figure 8.5

Action begins when Player 1 runs to Ball 1, picks it up, and throws to Player 2. She then runs to Ball 2, picks it up, and throws it to Player 3. Player 1 turns and races full speed to where she picked up Ball 1. Player 2 tosses her a high fly ball. After catching the ball, she sets it on the ground. Player 1 turns around and runs to where she picked up Ball 2. Player 3 tosses her a high fly ball. After the catch, she sets it on the ground.

Players switch places after five rounds. Player 1 becomes Player 2, Player 2 becomes Player 3, and so on.

Four-Player Games

Full Circle

Four players go to an open field. Each brings a ball with her. Players stand about 40 feet apart (Figure 8.6).

Action starts when Player 1 sets her ball on the ground and takes off running toward Player 2. When she passes Player 2, Player 2 shouts "Now" and throws a ball high into the air. Player 1 catches the ball and makes a return throw to Player 2. Player 1 continues action

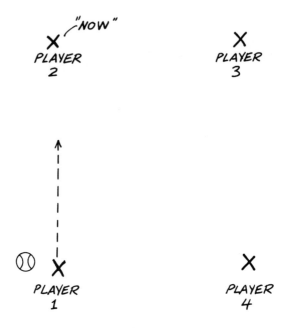

Figure 8.6

by doing the same thing with Player 3 and Player 4. After returning the ball to Player 4, Player 1 runs to her original starting position and picks up her ball. Player 2 then sets her ball on the ground and runs toward Player 3, and so on.

Each athlete runs the circle two times. If a player drops the ball or makes a wild throw, she loses all points. The player with the most points after two rounds wins the game.

Go!

Four players go to an open field. Players 2, 3, and 4 bring a ball with them and stand about 60 feet apart (Figure 8.7).

Action begins when Player 2 yells "Go." Player 1 runs straight ahead. Player 2 tosses Player 1 a fast-moving ground ball. Player 1 fields, turns, and throws to Player 3. Player 1 breaks to her left and runs deep. Player 3 throws a high fly into the air. Player 1 catches the ball and makes a return throw to Player 3. Then Player 1 runs full speed toward Player 4. Player 4 tosses a soft line drive to Player 1. Player 1 catches the ball and makes a return throw to Player 4. Player

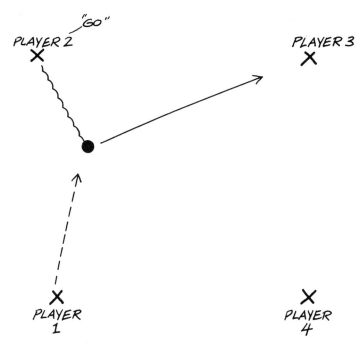

Figure 8.7

1 sprints to her starting position and repeats the procedure two more times. Player 1 must keep moving. She should run the pattern as fast as possible.

After three rounds players switch positions. Player 1 becomes Player 2, Player 2 becomes Player 3, and so on. The athlete with the most points wins.

TIPS AND SUGGESTIONS FOR PLAYING THE OUTFIELD

Here are additional tips and suggestions for you to pass along to your outfielders:

1. Hustle on and off the field. Play aggressive softball by staying heads up, backing up every throw possible, and getting rid of the ball quickly.

2. Warm up properly. Do not make unnecessary hard throws. Keep your arm (and body) fresh and strong.

3. Practice constantly on fielding grounders, line drives, and fly balls. Seek to improve your fielding ability.

4. Observe opposing batters. It is to your advantage to know the hitting ability of the girl swinging the bat.

5. Test wind conditions by throwing grass or paper into the air. If the wind is blowing toward the infield, take two or three steps closer to the infielders. If the wind is blowing toward the outfield, take two or three steps backward. A crosswind will cause a fly ball or a thrown ball to curve.

6. Place your body in a throwing position when attempting to field ground balls, line drives, or fly balls. This will help you get rid of the ball quickly.

7. Stay in constant communication with fellow teammates. A strong voice, in many cases, can prevent two players from colliding. For example, on a blooper hit into shallow left field, the shortstop (or third baseman) usually runs after the ball with her back facing the oncoming left fielder. If nobody warns them, the players may crash into each other and sustain major injuries.

   Undoubtedly, smooth communication between players minimizes confusion and allows athletes to work together in a harmonious manner.

   As an outfielder, clear communication becomes vitally important in these situations:

   • When you want other outfielders to know how you plan to player the batter. For instance, if the batter carries a "heavy hitter" reputation, you might shout to the nearest outfielder, "I'll play deep, you take anything short."

   • When you intend to field a batted ball, holler, "I've got it!" to ward off nearby players.

   • When discussing game conditions with other players—number of outs, inning, score, special game situations, and, if applicable, the wind factor.

   • When you shout instructions to a teammate making a play. For instance, "Throw to third" or "Fire it home."

   • When you say words of encouragement such as "Nice throw," "great catch," and so forth.

8. When fielding grounders keep your eyes fixed on the ball, stay low, and position your body in front of the ball.

9. Use both hands to field grounders, line drives, and fly balls.

10. Use a cross-seam grip when throwing the ball.

11. Finish off an overhand throw with a complete follow-through.

12. Keep throws one base ahead of the runner.

13. Expect every batted ball to come to you. When it does, you'll be able to get a good jump, field the ball, and throw it to the proper player.

14. Be mentally and physically ready at all times.

15. Think "Field" first, "Throw" second. In other words, the throw doesn't mean a thing unless you first field the ball. When fielding a slow bouncer coming straight at you, move in quickly and pick it up on the "long hop." The long hop is the bounce at its highest point. If that's not possible, try to pick it up on the "short hop." The short hop comes after the ball hits the ground. Try not to field the ball "between hops." A between hop is when the ball hits the ground between three to eight feet in front of you and is several inches above the ground.

16. On a ball that sails over your head, you must decide, turn, and quickly run to the spot where you think the ball will land. At the last moment look up, find, and catch the ball.

17. Constantly seek improvement. Never be satisfied with an adequate performance. Strive to be the best athlete you possibly can.

POINTS TO REMEMBER

Remind athletes that the outfield is no place for a clown or someone who wishes to lay back and take it easy. As successful outfielders, they must be good fielders, have strong, accurate throwing arms, and be able to make quick decisions.

Tell them that playing the outfield requires steady concentration, a knowledge of the opposition's hitting power and running speed, and a cooperative attitude.

Encourage outfielders to work on their own whenever they can. Give them drills and activities to do. Urge them to concentrate on their weak areas.

Many athletes make the mistake of practicing only their strong points, sidestepping problem areas. They do this because they want to look good in practice. Unfortunately, they make little or no progress. Therefore, when you spot an error in fielding or throwing, make sure the player realizes the problem and has a practice plan to remediate the situation.

9. Defensive Team Play

ONCE ATHLETES SETTLE into their playing positions, the next step is to bring them together and practice defensive strategy.

This chapter will cover the following areas:

1. Guidelines for setting up practice sessions
2. Cut-off and relay patterns
3. Pop-up assignments
4. Wild pitch assignments
5. Bunt plays
6. Rundown plays
7. Fast-action defensive drills
8. Points to remember

GUIDELINES FOR SETTING UP PRACTICE SESSIONS

As the season gets under way, you will readily spot the major weakspots that plague your defense. Practice games, intra-squad contests, and workout sessions reveal problem areas. Once you diagnose the situation, your next move is to set up specific steps for remediation. Here's a practice plan:

1. Identify the problem area; i.e., poor base coverage on bunt situations.

2. Select an activity or drill that stresses proper base coverage.

3. Go over the activity with athletes. Make sure they understand the purpose of the activity and the roles they play.

4. Practice hard. Be patient. Repeat the activity until the problem disappears.

5. Concentrate on one area at a time. Trying to solve too many problems in a single session tends to confuse athletes.

The next five sections will deal exclusively with team defensive-play situations. An introduction or suggested guidelines will precede each discussion.

CUT-OFF AND RELAY PATTERNS

Pass these tips along to your players:

- In all play situations, keep each base covered where there is a chance of making a play.

- The cut-off person must think quickly and figure out plays instantly, and must decide which runner is most important to cut down or put out. She cuts off throws to make possible the sure put-out, especially when the runner put out is the tying or the winning run. Throws to the cut-off person should be low enough for her to handle.

- Infielders should station themselves inside a base while watching the runners tag the base in making the turn. Being inside the base has a tendency to make the runner take a wider turn at the base, thus increasing the distance she travels toward the next base. Caution must be exercised not to interfere with the runner by being too close to the base.

- On routine fly balls to the outfield with no one on base, the outfielders should keep their throws low and to the glove side of the second baseman. The second baseman should cover when possible on all balls hit to left and center field; the shortstop should cover on balls hit to right field.

- The first and third baseman and the pitcher must always be ready to cover a throw that gets away from the catcher (covering home).

Now let's examine the player responsibilities for the following 21 defensive situations.

Situation #1:
Single to Left Field, No One on Base

Pitcher: Move to a position halfway between the mound and 2nd base to help cover for wild throws.

Catcher: Follow runner down to first base. Back up throw if it goes to first.

First Baseman: Make sure the runner tags the base in making the turn, then cover first base. Back up throw to second base.

Second Baseman: Cover second to take throw from left fielder.

Third Baseman: Protect third-base area.

Shortstop: Go for ball; outfielder is in control and has final call.

Center Fielder: Back up left fielder.

Right Fielder: Move in toward first-base area to back up throw.

Situation #2:
Single to Left Field, Runner on First

Pitcher: Back up third base.

Catcher: Protect home-plate area.

First Baseman: Cover first base.

Second Baseman: Cover second base.

Third Baseman: Cover third base.

Shortstop: Go for ball. Move into position to be the cut-off on throw to third base.

Center Fielder: Back up left fielder.

Right Fielder: Move in toward infield area. Back up throw if it goes to second.

Situation #3:
Single to Left Field, Man on Second, First and Second, or Bases Loaded

Pitcher: Cut off to home plate.

Catcher: Cover home plate.

First Baseman: Cover first base and cover down first-base side in case ball gets away from catcher or is a wild throw.

Second Baseman: Cover second base.

Third Baseman: Cover third base. If ball gets away from catcher or is a wild throw, go for ball.

Shortstop: Go for ball and then help cover third base if third baseman has to leave base.

Center Fielder: Back up left fielder.

Right Fielder: Move in toward second-base area.

Situation #4:
Single to Left Field (Judgment Play), Runner on Second Base; Hitter Is the Tying Run

Pitcher: Move off the mound and be cut-off to home plate in case the left fielder makes the throw home. Be ready to back up throw if ball goes to second.

Catcher: Cover home plate.

First Baseman: Cover first base. Be ready to back up throw if ball goes to second.

Second Baseman: Cover second base.

Third Baseman: Cover third base.

Shortstop: Go for ball.

Left Fielder: Make a low throw to second base to keep batter from advancing into scoring position. Never let the tying run get into scoring position at second base by making a foolish throw to the plate.

Center Fielder: Move into position to help back up left field.

Right Fielder: Move into position to help back up second base.

Situation #5:
Double, Possible Triple to Left-Center; No One on Base, Runner on Third or Second Base, or on Third and Second Base

Pitcher: Back up third base in line with the throw.

Catcher: Protect home plate.

First Baseman: Ease down first-base line. Be ready for bad throw or to help around home plate.

Second Baseman: Cover second base.

Third Baseman: Cover third base; stand on left-field side of bag.

Shortstop: Go to a spot in left-center to become relay man.

Center Fielder: Back up the left fielder.

Right Fielder: Move in toward second base. Back up second in case of a throw.

Situation #6:
Double, Possible Triple to Left Center; Man on First and Second, or Bases Loaded

Pitcher: Go halfway between home and third and then back up third or act as a cut-off if throw goes home.

Catcher: Protect home plate.

First Baseman: Come down first-base side. Be ready for bad throw and help around home plate area.

Second Baseman: Cover second base.

Third Baseman: Cover third base; stand on left-field side of bag.

Shortstop: Go to a spot in left-center to become relay person.

Center Fielder: Back up left fielder.

Right Fielder: Move in to back up second base.

Situation #7:
Double, Possible Triple, Down Left Field Foul Line; Runner on First Base

Pitcher: Cut-off for home.

Catcher: Cover home plate.

First Baseman: Back up home plate.

Second Baseman: Cover second base.

Third Baseman: Cover third base.

Shortstop: Relay person.

Center Fielder: Back up left fielder.

Right Fielder: Back up second base.

Situation #8:
Single to Center Field; No One on Base

Pitcher: Move to a position halfway between the mound and second base.

Catcher: Protect home-plate area.

First Baseman: Make sure the runner tags the base in making the turn, then cover first base.

Second Baseman: Cover second base if ball is on shortstop side. If the ball is on the second-base side, go for ball.

Third Baseman: Protect third base area.

Shortstop: Cover second to take throw from center fielder if ball is on the second-base side. If ball is hit on shortstop side, go for ball.

Left and Right Fielders: Back up center fielder.

Situation #9:
Single to Center Field; Runner on First

Pitcher: Back up third base.

Catcher: Protect home plate.

First Baseman: Cover first base.

Second Baseman: Cover second base.

Third Baseman: Cover third base.

Shortstop: Be cut-off person on throw from center field to third base.

Left and Right Fielders: Back up center fielder.

Situation #10:
Single to Center Field; Runner on Second Base, or Second and Third Bases

Pitcher: Be the cut-off person.

Catcher: Cover home plate.

First Baseman: Back up home plate.

Second Baseman: Go after ball. If possible, return to cover first base.

Third Baseman: Cover third base.

Shortstop: Go after ball, then cover second base.

Left Fielder: Back up center fielder.

Right Fielder: Back up center fielder.

Situation #11:
Single to Center Field; Runners on First and Second, or Bases Loaded

Pitcher: Go halfway between home and third base and then back up at third base. If throw goes home, be cut-off.

Catcher: Cover home plate.

First Baseman: If throw goes to third base, hustle back to first base to cover that bag. If throw goes home, be backup at home.

Second Baseman: Cover second base.

Third Baseman: Cover third base.

Shortstop: Go for the ball. Be the cut-off person for a possible throw to third.

Left and Right Fielder: Back up center fielder.

Situation #12:
Fly Ball to Center Field or Right Field; Runners on First and Third, or Bases Loaded

Pitcher: Be cut-off for home.

Catcher: Cover home plate.

First Baseman: Be backup for throw home. Cover base if runner is off too far.

Second Baseman: Go for ball if shallow. If deep, start for ball then cover first.

Third Baseman: Cover third base.

Shortstop: Go for ball if shallow. If deep, start for ball then go back and cover second.

Left Fielder: Move toward fly ball. If it stays in center field area, move toward third.

Right Fielder: Move toward fly ball.

Situation #13:
Single to Right Field; No One on Base

Pitcher: Move to a position halfway between the mound and second base.

Catcher: Protect home plate area.

First Baseman: Make sure the runner tags the base in making the turn, then cover first base.

Second Baseman: Go for ball.

Third Baseman: Protect third-base area. Be ready for bad throw.

Shortstop: Cover second.

Center Fielder: Back up right fielder.

Left Fielder: Move in toward third base. Be ready to back up throw to second.

Situation #14:
Single to Right Field; Runner on First or First and Second

Pitcher: Back up third base in line with throw.

Catcher: Protect home plate.

First Baseman: Cover first base. Make sure runner tags first base. Be ready for throw.

Second Baseman: Go for the ball.

Third Baseman: Cover third base.

Shortstop: Cover second. If throw is going to third, act as cut-off.

Left Fielder: Move in toward third base.

Center Fielder: Back up right fielder.

Right Fielder: May be able to throw out runner at second or runner at first.

Situation #15:
Single to Right Field; Runner on Second Base or Runners on Second and Third Bases

Pitcher: Act as cut-off.

Catcher: Cover home plate.

First Baseman: Cover first. Be ready to help at home.

Second Baseman: Go for the ball then cover first base.

Third Baseman: Cover third base. Be ready to help at home.

Shortstop: Cover second base.

Left Fielder: Move in toward third base.

Center Fielder: Back up right fielder.

Situation #16:
Single to Right Field, Between First and Second Base; Runner on Second Base, or Runners on Second and Third Bases

Pitcher: Start to cover first; then act as cut-off for home plate.

Catcher: Cover home plate.

First Baseman: After attempting to field ball, cover first.

Second Baseman: After attempting to field ball, go back to second base.

Third Baseman: Cover third. Be ready if throw gets away from catcher.

Shortstop: Cover second, then third.

Left Fielder: Move into area behind third base. Be ready to cover third if needed.

Center Fielder: Back up right fielder; move in toward second base after ball is fielded.

Situation #17:
Single to Right Field; Runners on First and Second or Bases Loaded

Pitcher: Cut off throw to home. If throw goes to third, back up third base.

Catcher: Cover home plate.

First Baseman: Go for ball. Cover first, then be ready in case of bad throw.

Second Baseman: Go for ball, then go back to second base.

Third Baseman: Cover third base.

Shortstop: Cover second base; act as cut-off person for the throw to third base. Then go back up third.

Left Fielder: Move to a point near the line and back up third base.

Center Fielder: Back up right fielder, then back up second base.

Right Fielder: Make a low throw to the pitcher or shortstop to keep the tying or winning run from going on to third base.

Situation #18:
Double, Possible Triple to Right Center Field, No One on Base, Runners on Third or Second, or Runners on Third and Second

Pitcher: Back up third base. Get as deep as possible.

Catcher: Protect home plate.

First Baseman: Move in toward infield, be ready.

Second Baseman: Go to spot in center field in line with third to become relay person.

Third Baseman: Cover third base.

Shortstop: Cover second.

Left Fielder: Move in toward third base.

Right Fielder: Back up center fielder. Then back up second base.

Situation #19:
Double, Possible Triple to Right Center Field; Runners on First Base, Runners on First and Second Bases, or Bases Loaded

Pitcher: Act as cut-off for home. If throw goes to third, back up third base.

Catcher: Cover home plate.

First Baseman: Move in toward home to back up.

Second Baseman: Become relay person.

Third Baseman: Cover third base. Be ready to cover bad throw to home plate.

Shortstop: Cover second base.

Left Fielder: Move into area behind third base.

Center Fielder: Go after the ball. Then back up bases.

Right Fielder: Go after the ball. Then back up bases.

Situation #20:
Double, Possible Triple Down the Right Field Line; No One on Base

Pitcher: Back up third.

Catcher: Protect home-plate area.

First Baseman: Move in toward infield. Be ready.

Second Baseman: Become relay person.

Third Baseman: Cover third base.

Shortstop: Cut-off to third. Be ready to cover second base.

Left Fielder: Move into an area behind third base.

Center Fielder: Back up right fielder.

Situation #21:
Double, Possible Triple, Down Right Field Line; Runner on First Base

Pitcher: Go half way between third and home to see where throw is going.

Catcher: Cover home plate.

First Baseman: Cut-off for throw to home.

Second Baseman: Relay person. Go to a spot in right field along foul lines in line with right fielder and home.

Third Baseman: Cover third base.

Shortstop: Cover second base.

Left Fielder: Move in toward third base.

Center Fielder: Back up right fielder.

POP-UP ASSIGNMENTS

Make sure your athletes understand these basic maneuvers:

- An infield pop fly will be all infielders' responsibility, and they must try for the ball until one fielder takes charge by calling for the play. When calling, yell loudly three or four times.

- Each infielder has her area, but she may take the play out of her area if she has taken charge of the play. Do not call for the ball too soon, especially on windy days.

- On questionable pop flies around the mound area, and after one or more infielders call for the ball, have the pitcher call the name of the fielder she thinks is in the best position to make the play.

- All pop flies directly behind the first and third basemen will be the responsibility of the second baseman and the shortstop.

Situation #1:
A foul fly is hit behind the plate on the first base side; runners on first and third with less than two out. Both runners tag up and the runner on first breaks for second. If there is no cut-off man, the runner on third will score easily when the throw is made to second base.

Pitcher: Cover home plate.

Catcher: Catch pop-up and throw to cut-off person if runner breaks.

First Baseman: Help on pop-up. Then back up first base for possible throw from shortstop.

Second Baseman: Cover first base.

Third Baseman: Cover third base.

Shortstop: Cover second base. If runner breaks from third on the throw from the catcher, move in to cut off the throw and relay to home.

Left Fielder: Come in to help back up the third-base area.

Center Fielder: Back up the second-base area.

Right Fielder: Back up the first-base area.

Situation #2:
A pop fly is hit behind first base; runners on first and third with no outs. Both runners tag up and the runner on first breaks for second.

Pitcher: Come to a point in the first-base area to be the cut-off person.

Catcher: Cover home plate.

First Baseman: Catch the pop-up and throw to the pitcher.

Second Baseman: Also go after the pop-up; then hustle to cover first base.

Third Baseman: Cover third base.

Shortstop: Cover second base.

Left Fielder: Move into an area behind third to back up.

Center Fielder: Back up second base.

Right Fielder: Move in to help with the pop-up.

WILD PITCH ASSIGNMENTS

Situation #1:
Runner on Third, First, and Third, or Runners on First, Second, and Third

Pitcher: Cover home plate.

Catcher: Retrieve the ball.

First Baseman: Cover first-base side and back up throw to the plate.

Second Baseman: Cover second base.

Third Baseman: Cover third-base side and back up the throw to the plate.

Shortstop: Cover third base.

Outfielders: Move toward infield area and help out where needed.

BUNT PLAYS

Here are pointers to give your infielders regarding bunt situations:

Runner on First Base

- When you expect the sacrifice bunt, charge in when the pitcher throws the ball.

- If the ball is bunted hard to you, make the play to second base. The catcher will call this play.
- If play at second is doubtful, make sure you get one out by throwing to first base.

Runners on First and Second

- The third baseman's judgment is the key to this play. She takes complete charge.
- Tell the pitcher to field the ball. *Note:* One out must be made in this situation.
- When the pitcher fields the ball, the third baseman covers her bag without taking her eyes off the ball. She tags the base with her right foot for better balance and to be in position for a possible throw to first.
- On balls bunted down the line, the third baseman charges the ball and runs the pitcher off. The third baseman can handle the ball much easier than the pitcher.

Situation #1:
Runner on First

Pitcher: Break toward home plate after releasing the ball. Cover home if the catcher fields the ball.

Catcher: Field all bunts possible; call the play. Cover third when third baseman fields the bunt in close to home plate.

First Baseman: Cover the area between first and the mound. If third baseman covers bunt, then first baseman runs to cover third for the possible advance by the runner on first.

Second Baseman: Cover first base. Cheat by moving closer to first on the delivery of the pitch.

Third Baseman: Cover the area between third and the mound. If you do not field the ball, hustle back to cover third.

Shortstop: Cover second base.

Left Fielder: Be ready to cover third base.

Center Fielder: Back up second base.

Right Fielder: Back up first base.

Situation #2:
Runners on First and Second

Pitcher: Break toward third-base line after releasing the ball.

Catcher: Field bunts in front of the plate; call the play.

First Baseman: Be responsible for all balls in the area between first and a direct line from the mound to home.

Second Baseman: Cover first base.

Third Baseman: Take position, then cover third.

Shortstop: Cover second base.

Left Fielder: Back up third base.

Center Fielder: Back up second base.

Right Fielder: Back up first base.

Situation #3:
Runners on First and Second

Pitcher: Break toward the plate.

Catcher: Field bunts in front of plate or call the play.

First Baseman: Charge toward the plate.

Second Baseman: Cover first base.

Third Baseman: Charge toward the plate.

Shortstop: Cover third base.

Outfielders: Move in toward infield area on all bunt situations.

RUNDOWN PLAYS

Go over the following guidelines with your athletes:

- Run the runner back to the bag from which she came.
- Try to start this play when the runner is halfway between the bases.
- Give the ball to the forward player, and let her run the runner back to the bag from which she came.
- The forward player should run hard at the runner, but not with a faking motion of the arm.
- The tagger should stay in front of her bag and inside the baseline. This will give her the proper angle on the throw.
- When the runner is about ten feet from the tagger, the tagger should make a break toward the runner. This is the sign to the thrower to give the tagger the ball on her first step.

- The thrower makes an easy, chest-high toss.
- When the play is worked right, one throw is all that is needed to get the runner at any base.
- The player without the ball must avoid interfering with the runner.

Situation #1:
Runner on First and Second, Runner on First Gets Picked Off

Pitcher: Back up first base.

Catcher: Cover home plate.

First Baseman: Cover first and be the tag person.

Second Baseman: Cover second base and be the rundown person.

Third Baseman: Cover third to keep runner on second from advancing.

Shortstop: Back up and cover second base with possibility of being run-down person or tagger.

Left Fielder: Come in to help back up third.

Center Fielder: Come in to help back up second.

Right Fielder: Come in to help back up first.

Situation #2:
Runners on First and Second, Runner on Second Gets Picked Off

Pitcher: Back up third base.

Catcher: Cover home plate.

First Baseman: Cover first base.

Second Baseman: Cover second base with the possibility of being the run-down person or tagger.

Third Baseman: Cover third base and be the rundown person.

Shortstop: Cover second base and be the tagger.

Left Fielder: Move into area behind third to back up play.

Center Fielder: Back up second base.

Right Fielder: Back up second base.

Situation #3:
Runner on First and Third, Runner on Third Gets Picked Off

Pitcher: Cover home plate and back up catcher.

Catcher: Cover home plate and be the rundown person.

First Baseman: Cover first base to keep runner there from advancing.

Second Baseman: Cover second base to keep runner there from advancing.

Third Baseman: Cover third base and be the tag person.

Shortstop: Back up the third baseman.

Left Fielder: Move in behind third base to help back up.

Center Fielder: Move into position to back up second base.

Right Fielder: Move in to help back up second base. May be involved in rundown.

Situation #4:
Runner on Third Tries to Score on Ground Ball, Infield Playing In

Pitcher: Cover home plate. Back up.

Catcher: Cover home plate and be the rundown person.

First Baseman: Cover first base.

Second Baseman: Cover second base.

Third Baseman: Follow in about ten feet behind runner off third to make tag quickly. This will keep batter from going to second base.

Shortstop: Cover third base.

Left Fielder: Back up third base.

Center Fielder: Back up second base.

Right Fielder: Back up area behind first base.

FAST-ACTION DEFENSIVE DRILLS

Defensive drills, using extra players as runners, gives you a chance to create game conditions and stop play to make adjustments. Here are four fast-moving drills to help ready your team for competition:

Nine Outs

Objective: To practice strengthening defensive skills.

Procedure: Divide the team into two equal groups, Team A and Team B, nine players per team.

Team A takes the field; Team B players come to home plate, form a single line, and act as runners. Have athletes wear protective headgear when running the bases.

The coach, acting as a hitter, comes to home plate with a bat and ball. The first runner in line stands about three feet away and parallel to home plate.

Action begins when the pitcher winds up and releases the ball. As soon as it hits the catcher's mitt, the coach fungoes somewhere in the field. The runner takes off and plays the ball accordingly. Athletes are expected to hustle and give 100 percent.

After three outs, clear the bases of runners and begin play over again. Sides change after nine outs. The team scoring the most runs in the allotted time wins. Have the losing team carry in the equipment after practice. The coach's fungoing ability, in most cases, determines which team will win.

Set Up

Objective: To practice strengthening defensive skills.

Procedure: The same as "Nine Outs." This time, however, you set up the situation by stationing runners on base before fungoing the ball. For example, you might say, "Runners go to first and second, no outs." You then hit the ball somewhere in the field. You control the tempo of the game by moving runners around at will.

Fast Out

Objective: To practice strengthening defensive skills.

Procedure: Divide the team into two equal groups, Team A and Team B, nine players per team.

Team A takes the field; Team B players come to bat. Each athlete on Team B receives one pitch to make contact with the ball.

Action begins when the first player in line steps up to the plate. She receives one pitch and must hit the ball somewhere in fair territory. If the pitcher fails to throw a strike, the batter walks. If the batter swings and misses or fouls off the pitch, she is out.

After nine outs (optional), the coach clears the bases of runners and sides change. The team scoring the most runs in the allotted time wins. Allow athletes to use prearranged signals to score runs.

Set Score

Objective: To practice strengthening defensive skills.

Procedure: The same as "Fast Out" with one exception: Team B comes to bat behind in the score with nine outs (optional) in which to win the round. For example, the coach says, "Team A, 4 runs; Team B, no runs." Now the pressure is on Team B to score five runs before making nine outs.

After nine outs (optional), clear the bases of runners and sides change. The team winning the most rounds (18 outs per round) in the allotted time wins.

POINTS TO REMEMBER

A good time to schedule defensive drill activities is the day before a game. This gives you a chance to set defensive strategy and prepare athletes accordingly. Keeping everybody active and making on-the-spot corrections readies athletes mentally and physically.

Athletes will respond favorably to team defensive drills if you keep them moving briskly, keep the activities competitive, and show an enthusiastic spirit throughout practice.

10. The Running Game

WHEN A PLAYER becomes a runner she must turn her thoughts to scoring any way she can. She may score with one swing of the bat or slide once or twice before touching home plate.

Intelligent baserunning requires an athlete to stay alert and take advantage of defensive mistakes. A heady base runner slides into bases to avoid colliding with the fielder or to beat the throw.

We'll examine the following areas in this chapter:

1. Developing a successful running game
2. Setting up running situations
3. Baserunning drills
4. Examining three sliding techniques
5. Fast-action sliding drills
6. Tips and suggestions for baserunning and sliding
7. Points to remember

DEVELOPING A SUCCESSFUL RUNNING GAME

You can build a running ball club from athletes with average speed. You may have only one or two speedsters, so your success might well depend on how fast your athletes think and react.

You Can Instill Player Confidence and Get Your Athletes to Think Hustle by Doing These Things:

- Encourage base runners to take a chance rather than hold back on questionable plays. Common sense, of course, should prevail and guide players accordingly. You wouldn't want an athlete to risk an out by taking an extra base, especially if your team is three runs behind.

- A running ball club forces the opposition to make mistakes. Fielders often lose concentration and hurry their throws when they think a runner will take an extra base. Put pressure on the opponent's defense by keeping them guessing.

- Teach aggressive baserunning. Convince athletes that a heads-up, hard-sliding player earns respect from her opponents as well as teammates.

- Praise each athlete's running ability. Recognize and reward a tough effort. The slowest runner on the team will go all out if she knows her coach truly appreciates her determination.

- Make running the bases an integral part of practice. Some coaches begin and end practice by having athletes run the bases. For example:
  First ten minutes of practice—athletes circle the bases, sprint down the first base line, and sprint from home plate to second base.
  Last ten minutes of practice—athletes steal second base, score from second base, and circle the bases.

- Stress running without hesitation; i.e., once an athlete decides to do something, she must carry through with her plan. A delay or break in rhythm can cause a sliding runner to seriously injure herself.

- Practice the essential components of the running game every day. Hold bunting, running, and sliding drills in a gamelike atmosphere. Athletes try harder when they compete against each other.

SETTING UP RUNNING SITUATIONS

Let's look at four running situations and how you can use them in practice.

Straight Steal

A runner can get a fast takeoff from any base by using the rocker step. It works like this:

- The runner places her left foot on the outfield-side of the bag (Figure 10.1).

- She brings her right foot behind the left foot in a semi-sprinter's start position.

- As the pitcher goes into motion, the runner rocks back and steps forward when the pitcher's arm comes down. The left foot will come off base as pitcher releases ball.

A batter must distract the catcher in any legal manner. A batter can do two things to give the base runner an extra second or two. They are: (1) Stand as far back in the batter's box as possible without making the steal look too obvious; or (2) bring bat down in bunting position. As the pitch comes across home plate, draw bat straight back as if trying to avoid bunting the ball.

Figure 10.1

Rock and Go

Objective: To practice the rocker-step takeoff.

Procedure: Divide the squad into two groups, Team A and Team B. Team A athletes, defense, alternate playing catcher, batter, pitcher, and second base. Team B, runners, line up near first base.

Action begins when the pitcher begins her windup. The runner rocks back and steps forward. The batter, standing deep in the batter's box, squares around to bunt. When the pitcher releases the ball, the runner breaks for second, and the batter draws her bat back at the last moment. The catcher throws to second.

Runners should go full speed and slide into the bag. Keep a player in short center to shag misplayed balls. Change sides after each runner receives four chances to steal.

Note: The coach should stand behind the pitcher's mound. This gives the coach an excellent view of the entire play.

Bunt and Run

This play involves trying to advance the runner from first to third on a sacrifice bunt. The batter must:

- Get the bat on the ball and bunt it on the ground.
- Square around early and keep her eyes fixed on the ball.
- Stay in the batter's box until she sees the ball hit the ground.
- Bunt the ball toward the third baseman, if possible.
- Make every attempt to bunt the ball. If the ball cannot be bunted, the batter should protect the runner by fouling the pitch or distracting the catcher.

The runner plays the situation as a straight steal except she runs while watching the batter. If the batter pops the ball up, the runner returns to first. If the batter misses the pitch, the runner goes to second.

When the bunted ball touches the ground, the runner looks at third base. If nobody is covering third, the runner sprints around second and heads for third. If the third baseman stays close to her bag, the runner stops at second.

Bunt/Run

Objective: To advance the base runner.

Procedure: Divide the squad into two groups, Team A and Team B. Team A athletes, defense, alternate playing catcher, pitcher, and infield. Team B, offense, take turns bunting and running.

Action begins when a Team B player goes to first (runner) and another grabs a bat and comes to home plate. The batter attempts to bring the runner around to third by bunting the ball down the third-base line. After the batter bunts the ball, she becomes runner. The runner goes to the end of the line and waits her turn to bunt the ball. Sides change after eight or ten minutes and play continues.

Note: The coach can make defensive adjustments and correct mistakes as they occur. The coach should stand in foul territory between home plate and third base.

First and Third

Situation: Runner on third; batter walks. After she walks, have the batter round first and go immediately to second. Tell her to move toward second cautiously if the pitcher has the ball in circle. Instruct the runner to bait the pitcher into making a throw to second. Have the runner stay in a rundown long enough to allow the runner on third to score. If the pitcher doesn't throw to second, the runner should stay close to the bag.

The runner on third must return quickly to the bag if the pitcher takes the catcher's throw while standing in the circle. The runner on third must be ready to sprint home on the coach's command or whenever a fielder bobbles the ball or is out of position to make a throw home.

Most teams allow the runner at first to reach second without a play, thus eliminating a bad throw in a rundown.

The runner at first can bait the pitcher into throwing the ball by walking in a brisk manner toward second. Also, a delayed steal may draw a throw from the catcher.

First/Third

Objective: To score the runner from third.

Procedure: Have infielders take their positions. Divide remaining players into two groups, A and B. Send Group A to home plate; Group B to third base. Both groups act as runners. A Group A athlete goes to home plate; a Group B player goes to third.

Action starts when the pitcher delivers a ball to the catcher. The coach, standing in foul territory between third and home, yells "Ball Four." Runner A trots to first, rounds the bag, and walks toward second. Have the pitcher throw the ball. Now your athletes can work on defense and offense at the same time.

Move players about during the drill. Have them practice running and fielding. This is a good time to set your defense against the first and third situation.

Delayed Steal

A runner may try a delayed steal when she sees an opportunity to take an extra base or when she receives a prearranged signal from the coach. This play can be effective against pitchers, catchers, and infielders that fail to check runners after every pitch. A lob toss back to the pitcher from the catcher gives a runner a great head start!

On a delayed steal the runner must react quickly and fire out without hesitation. Encourage athletes to attempt a delayed steal when:

- The catcher lobs the ball back to the pitcher.
- The pitcher turns her back to the runner after receiving the ball from the catcher.
- Infielders aren't paying close attention to the runners. They fail to cover their bases after each pitch.

One way to have athletes practice getting an explosive start from base is to play "Time Bomb." Simply mark off a distance, say 30 feet, from first base. Have athletes form a line near the bag. Each player, in turn, comes to first base and assumes a semi-sprinter's stance. On the command "Go" the runner has a certain time to fire out and reach the marked distance or . . . boom. She loses, returns to the line, and pays a penalty (push-ups, sit-ups, etc.).

BASERUNNING DRILLS

What does it take to be a good base runner? Most successful runners agree that concentration and constant practice are the main ingredients; a runner with average speed can become a threat on the base paths.

The following drills will help your athletes refine their baserunning skills:

Circle 'Em

Objective: To give players practice in rounding the bases.

Procedure: Give athletes this information: When you approach first base, veer to the right and shift body weight slightly to that side. Then start an arc that will cut the inside corner of the base (touch the base with either foot, shift weight back to that side, and push off the base) and head for second. The runner should continue rounding each base with the same arc she started at first base.

Action begins when all players line up near home plate. Each player, in turn, swings at an imaginary pitch and runs the bases. Repeat several times.

Time Run

Objective: To record the speed of each player.

Procedure: Athletes line up near home plate. Each player, in turn, swings at an imaginary pitch and runs to first. She returns to the end of the line. The coach records each runner's speed from home to first, first to second, and second to home.

Game Simulation (Six-part drill)

Objective: To practice hitting, bunting, and running in a gamelike atmosphere.

Procedure: Break the team into two groups, A and B. Group A takes the field; Group B comes to home plate.

Action begins when the pitcher delivers the ball. The coach gives the batter a prearranged bunt signal. The signal tells the batter the type of bunt—sacrifice or base hit—and where to drop the bunt—down the first or third baseline. The batter stays at first even if the throw beats her (Part 1).

The runner steals second base on the next pitch. The batter attempts to legally distract the catcher (Part 2).

The batter swings away at the next pitch in the strike zone. The runner's job is to score from second base. No matter where the batter hits the ball the runner scores from second. This allows the runner a chance to react to the pitcher's motion and take off when the ball hits the bat (Part 3).

After reaching home, the runner goes to the end of the line. The next player in line becomes the batter. Regardless of where she hits the ball, she rounds first and stops at second base. The batter receives practice on exploding out of the batter's box, rounding first, and reaching second base safely. The infielders react to the ball and make a play at first base (Part 4).

The next athlete in line sacrifices the runner from second to third. The batter stays on first base (Part 5).

With runners on first and third, Group B can execute a double-squeeze play and have both runners going on the pitch. The batter, however, must concentrate on bunting the ball or fouling it off since the runner coming home intends to score (Part 6).

Bunt and Run

Objective: To practice the bunt and run play.

Procedure: Break the team into two groups, A and B. Group A takes the field; Group B splits into three smaller groups—Group 1, runners, goes to third base; Group 2, runners, goes to first base; Group 3, batters, goes to home plate.

Action begins when runners go to first and third and a batter steps up to the plate. The batter receives three chances to lay down a sacrifice bunt. When she bunts the ball, she runs to first, and then gets into the runners line at first.

The first-base runner sprints toward second and checks for the bunt. If the ball stays in fair territory, she goes to second. Prior to reaching the bag, she looks at third. If third base is open, she steps on the infield side of second, pushes off, and races to third base. If the batter misses the ball, the runner hustles back to first, diving head first if necessary.

The third-base runner practices the squeeze play as the ball contacts the bat.

After the play, first-base runners become third-base runners and third-base runners become batters.

EXAMINING THREE SLIDING TECHNIQUES

An aggressive base runner welcomes an opportunity to slide and possibly knock the ball out of the fielder's glove. For some players, however, the thought of sliding creates tension and takes the fun out of baserunning. Simply, these athletes are afraid to slide. As a coach, you must convince them that wearing the proper protection—long pants, sliding pads—plus learning (and practicing) the correct methods of sliding will reduce the risk of injury.

Let's begin by examining three popular sliding methods: Straight-on, hook, and bent-leg-and-up.

Offer these suggestions to your athletes:

Straight-on Slide

- Use either foot for takeoff.
- Bend takeoff foot to side after leaving the ground.
- Point the extended leg at the base (Figure 10.2). Keep front body weight shifted backward as you slide into the base.

Figure 10.2

Hook Slide

- Prior to starting your slide, decide which side of the bag, left or right, you will contact. *Caution:* Don't change your mind in the middle of the slide. Indecision leads to injury.
- Drop to the ground, bend both legs, and slide to the opposite side of the tag (Figure 10.3).
- The hooking leg is the takeoff or last leg to leave the ground. Once the runner reaches the ground, she slides on her hip. Her hands should be held back, out of the way.

Figure 10.3

Bent-Leg-and-Up

- The runner usually extends the first foot to leave the ground out in front of the body. *Note:* This slide can be made on either side of the bag.

- She bends the trailing foot under the knee of the extended leg. The slide is made in a sit-down position, the calf and hip of the bent leg contacting the ground. The extended leg is carried in the air (Figure 10.4).

- A runner's momentum brings her to her feet. She helps by pushing off the bag with her bent leg. Also, by hitting the bag with the extended foot, the runner quickly comes to her feet. This allows her to take an extra base if the throw gets by the fielder.

Figure 10.4

FAST-ACTION SLIDING DRILLS

Here is a simple warm-up activity to give athletes prior to sliding practice:

Bring athletes and two bases to a grassy area in the outfield. Set the bases about 20 feet apart. Have players form two lines (A and B), one line behind each base. The coach stands about 30 feet away and between the lines (Figure 10.5).

Have the first person in each line assume a semi-sprinter's stance. Action begins when the coach hollers "Rock, Go." On the command "Go" the runners break toward the coach. When the runners near the bases, the coach yells "Hit It." Line A runner slides to the left of the base; Line B runner slides to the right of the base. Runners return to opposite lines; i.e., Runner A goes to Line B and Runner

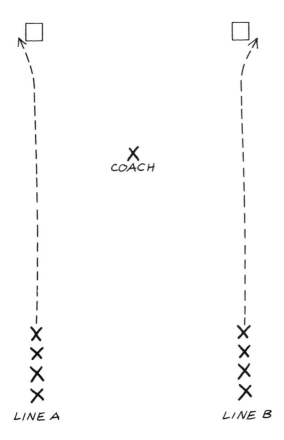

Figure 10.5

B goes to Line A. Every athlete should slide three or four times into each base.

You may wish to try the following fast-action running and sliding practice. It works like this:

1. Run the bases—all players run at the same time, starting at two-second intervals—*three minutes*
2. Presliding practice warm-up—*five minutes*
3. Hook slide/bent-leg-and-up—*ten minutes*
4. Two-Base Race—*ten minutes*

The sliding-practice session lasts approximately 30 minutes. It gives athletes a chance to move about and polish their sliding skills. It also allows the coach an opportunity to make on-the-spot corrections.

We've covered running the bases and setting up a presliding practice activity. Now let's see how to organize the hook slide/bent-leg-and-up drill, and two-base race drill.

Hook Slide, Bent-Leg-and-Up Drill

Objective: To practice strengthening sliding skills.

Procedure: Line athletes up near home plate. Each player, in turn, rounds first, hook slides into second, and comes to her feet. She then slides into third with a bent-leg-and-up, sprints home, and hook slides into the plate. The coach, standing near home plate, drops a glove or towel to one side of the plate. The runner slides into the target.

After each athlete runs the bases twice, repeat the drill. This time have the runners use a bent-leg-and-up at second and hook slide into third and home. For added interest, time each player around the bases.

Two-Base Race

Objective: To practice the straight-on and hook slide.

Procedure: Divide the team into two equal lines. Place two bases in a straight line ahead of each group. Place the first base 45 feet away from the first athlete in line and the second base 90 feet away (Figure 10.6). On "Go," the first player in each line races forward, slides straight-on into the first bag, jumps to her feet, runs to the second base, and hook slides to the left. She races back to the front of the line and tags the next girl. Repeat the procedure until every player receives a chance to slide. Each athlete takes two turns. The losing team pays by doing push-ups.

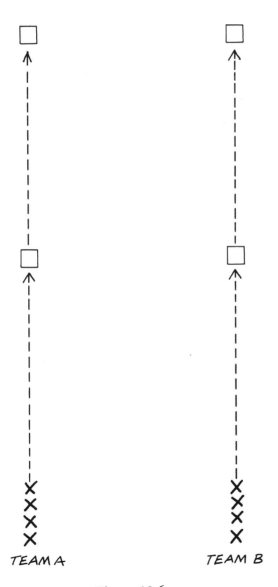

TEAM A   TEAM B

Figure 10.6

TIPS AND SUGGESTIONS
FOR BASERUNNING AND SLIDING

These reminders will help sharpen your athletes as they travel around the bases:

1. Keep moving briskly. Avoid hesitation and follow through with your original intent.

2. When running down the base path, follow a straight line. Do not change your pace and jump for the base at the last moment. You actually slow down when you leap for the bag.

3. Touch the inside of the bag and push off as you round the bases. This saves time and keeps your momentum going.

4. As you round the bases, approach each base in a slight arc, remembering to touch the inside corner.

5. Keep your head up, eyes open, and listen for your coach to guide you.

6. Know the throwing abilities of opposing players. Don't challenge a rifle arm when your team can't spare an out or if you aren't ready to slide hard into the base.

7. Practice sliding. Know when to begin your slide. An early slide may stop you short of the bag; a late slide may carry you past the bag and cause you to injure yourself.

8. Wear protective sliding pads and long-legged pants. It is a good idea to remove cleats before sliding practice.

9. Keep your eye on the ball as you run the bases. A bobbled ball or misplay may allow you to take an extra base.

10. The art of sliding makes good base runners out of average base runners.

POINTS TO REMEMBER

A hustling athlete motoring around the bases makes the game come alive. She often turns a slow bouncing ball into a base hit.

A player may have average speed, but she can develop into a topnotch base runner by practicing hard, listening to encouraging words, and keeping a check on her progress.

An athlete may improve her speed around the bases by getting a good jump out of the batter's box, hitting the inside corner of each base, pushing off hard, and leaning her weight toward the next base.

A base runner should have fair speed, be alert, and be ready to take an extra base. She should listen to and follow directions given by the base coaches. An intelligent base runner finds time to practice the correct methods of base running, sliding, and firing out of the batter's box.

11. Bunting

BUNTING, LIKE ANY OTHER SOFTBALL SKILL, demands concentrated practice. Too often an athlete elects to bypass bunting in favor of swinging away. Some athletes feel bunting is less important than hitting because they are seldom called upon to bunt.

Scoring the winning run with a perfectly placed bunt down the baseline is a thrilling experience for any athlete. Bunting, therefore, is the mainstay for a coach who believes in scoring one run at a time.

In this unit we will cover these topics:

1. The sacrifice bunt
2. Two-, three-, and four-player bunting drills
3. Small-group action drills
4. Bunting for the base hit
5. Base-hit bunting drills
6. Building confidence in bunting
7. Tips and suggestions for better bunting
8. Points to remember

THE SACRIFICE BUNT

The idea of a sacrifice bunt is to advance the baserunner(s) at the batter's expense. Therefore, a batter must drop the ball in fair territory, preferably near a base line.

Here are three methods of executing a sacrifice bunt (right-handed batter):

Square Around (hands held apart)

- Pivot on left foot; swing right foot around to face pitcher.
- Keep feet parallel, about shoulder width apart. Flex legs at the knees (Figure 11.1).
- Place left hand about two or three inches from the knob. Hold the middle of the bat between the thumb and index finger of right hand.
- Hold bat parallel to the ground, about shoulder high, arms fully extended, slightly flexed at the elbows.
- Keep head still, eyes fixed on the ball.
- The thumb and index finger of right hand give slightly as the ball hits the bat. This helps to "catch" the ball and drop it gently to the ground.
- Try to contact the ball on the fat or sweet part of the bat. Break for first *only* when the ball is bunted on the ground.

Figure 11.1

Square Around (hands held together)

- Pivot on left foot; swing right foot around to face pitcher.
- Keep feet parallel, about shoulder width apart. Flex legs at the knees.
- Grip the middle of the bat with both hands. Wrap the right hand around the trademark; place left hand next to the right hand (Figure 11.2).
- Hold bat parallel to the ground, about shoulder high, arms fully extended, slightly flexed at the elbows.
- Keep head still, eyes fixed on the ball.

Figure 11.2

Pivot Turn

- Make a quarter turn toward the pitcher by pivoting on both feet at the same time (Figure 11.3).
- Hold the bat, hands close together, about five or six inches from the knob.
- Hold the bat parallel to the ground out in front of home plate. Extend arms, flexing at the elbows.

- Lower body and shift weight over flexed right knee.
- Keep head still, eyes fixed on the ball.
- After bunting the ball on the ground, fire out of the batter's box by pushing hard off of the right foot.

Figure 11.3

TWO-, THREE-, AND FOUR-PLAYER BUNTING DRILLS

These small-group drills require minimum equipment and can be set up anywhere around the playing field. The objective of each drill is to refine bunting skills.

Two-Player Drills

Glove Bump

Procedure: Have two athletes go to an open area. Player 1, pitcher, stays about 40 feet away from Player 2, bunter. *Note:* Tell Player 2 to stand in front of a sideline fence, wall, or the backstop screen.

Action begins when Player 1 tosses her glove to her left or right side. She then delivers a pitch to Player 2. Player 2 squares and bunts the ball toward the glove. The idea is to bunt the ball on or near the target.

After six or eight bunts, athletes trade off and continue play. Partners should work together and correct each other's faults.

For added interest, set up a scoring system. Award two points if the ball touches the glove and stops rolling within three feet of the glove. Award one point if the ball stops rolling within three feet of the glove, but does not touch it. The athlete collecting the most points after three or four rounds wins. *Note:* Have pitchers concentrate on throwing strikes at one-half to three-quarter speed.

Called Direction

The procedure is the same as "Glove Bump" except the pitcher hollers "first baseline" or "third baseline" before delivering the ball. Player 2 bunts the ball in the called direction.

In this drill, have athletes earn one point for every properly bunted ball. To increase concentration, have bunter subtract one point from her point total every time she misses or fouls the pitch.

Three-Player Drills

Baseline Bunt

Procedure: Athletes bring two movable rubber bases to an open area. Bases, first and second, are set about 60 feet apart. Player 1, pitcher, stands between second base and Player 2, bunter. Player 3, runner, goes to first base.

Action begins when the pitcher delivers the ball. She doesn't move until Player 2 bunts the ball. However, as soon as the pitcher releases the ball, Player 3 sprints to second. She tries to reach second before the pitcher fields the ball. Player 2 concentrates on bunting the ball near the baseline.

After the play, the runner returns to first and action continues. The bunter acts as judge and determines whether or not Player 3 beat the play. Athletes switch positions after three bunts; i.e., Player 1 becomes Player 2, Player 2 becomes Player 3, and so on. Again, use any scoring system that keeps the drill moving at a brisk pace.

Double Toss

Procedure: Two athletes, Player 1 and Player 2, act as pitchers. They stand next to each other and stay about 40 feet away from Player 3, bunter. Both pitchers have a ball.

Action starts when Player 1, standing to the third base side of Player 2, delivers the ball. Two seconds later Player 2 releases a pitch. Player 3 bunts the first ball down the third baseline and the second ball down the first baseline.

After Player 3 bunts six balls, athletes rotate as they did in "Baseline Bunt."

Four-Player Drills

Two Left, Two Right

Procedure: Four athletes go to an open area. Players 1, 2, and 3 form a straight line and stay about ten feet apart. They stand approximately 40 feet away from Player 4, bunter.

Action begins when Player 2, pitcher, standing between Player 1 and Player 3, delivers the ball to Player 4. Player 4 bunts two pitches to Player 1 and two pitches to Player 3.

After bunting four balls, athletes rotate as they did in "Baseline Bunt."

Left, Right

Procedure: The procedure is the same as *Two Left, Two Right* except Player 1, standing near the third baseline, pitches the ball to Player 4, bunter.

After releasing the ball, Player 1 runs behind Player 4. Player 4 bunts the ball to the area vacated by Player 1. Player 2 breaks to her right and fields the ball.

After bunting the ball, Player 4 becomes Player 3, Player 3 becomes Player 2, Player 2 becomes Player 1, and Player 1 becomes the bunter.

After each athlete bunts the ball four times, switch direction. Now have Player 3, standing near the first baseline, pitch the ball and break behind Player 4. Player 4 bunts the ball to the area vacated by Player 3. Player 2 breaks to her left and fields the ball.

Player 4, after bunting the ball, becomes Player 1, and athletes rotate to the next position as they did before.

Small-Group Action Drills

The first two drills require five and six players respectively; the last drill makes use of two teams, six players per team. All activities require minimal equipment—rubber bases, bats, balls, and gloves. Catcher equipment is needed for the last drill. These activities will keep athletes on the move.

Bunt and Swing

Objective: To practice bunting, base running, and sliding.

Procedure: Five athletes go to an open area in the outfield near a fence or screen. They make a miniature playing field with rubber bases placed about 50 feet apart.

Athletes position themselves in the following manner:

Player 1—Pitcher; throws one-half to three-quarter speed.

Player 2—Baseman; plays near second base.

Player 3—Left-center fielder; plays medium deep. Plays left-center, medium deep.

Player 4—Right-center fielder; plays medium deep. Plays center-right, medium deep.

Player 5—Batter

The batter receives three swings. She must: (1) Bunt the first ball down the third baseline (batter stays at home plate); (2) bunt the second ball down the first baseline (batter stays at home plate); (3) hit the third ball somewhere in the outfield, run to first, round the base, and slide into second base. If the ball stays in the infield, the batter need only run to first.

Fielding players have the following responsibilities:

Player 1—Concentrates on throwing strikes. Fields all balls hit within her area; covers first base when Player 2 makes a play.

Player 2—Fields all balls hit to the left, right, and over the second base bag; covers first base when Player 1 makes a play.

Player 3—Fields all balls hit between the third baseline and center field.

Player 4—Fields all balls hit between center field and the first baseline.

After three swings, athletes rotate clockwise; for example, pitcher comes to bat, batter goes to left-center, left-center shifts to right-center, right-center moves to second base, and second baseman takes the mound.

Have athletes set up the following scoring system:

1 Point—For errors and every ball bunted into fair territory. Also, players who beat out ground balls for infield hits.

2 Points—Reaching second safely after hitting the third ball.

3 Points—Bunting the first and second ball into fair territory, down each baseline.

0 Points—Balls hit over the outfielders heads, bunted foul, or batters thrown out at first or second.

Athletes practice bunting balls down each baseline, punching the ball between outfielders, running the bases, and sliding into second base.

Precision Bunt

Objective: To practice bunting and running.

Procedure: Six players carry rubber bases, gloves, bats, and balls to an open area. They make a diamond, bases approximately 50 feet apart. Athletes divide into two teams, A and B, three players per team. Team A, offense, places a glove about 40 feet down each baseline. The gloves represent targets. Team B, defense, takes the field. One player goes to third, one to first, and the remaining athlete becomes a pitcher. Team A comes to the plate. Each batter receives one bunt per time at the bat.

Here are the rules:

- A batter may bunt the pitch anywhere on the diamond. She runs out every bunt. If the ball hits the baseline glove and bounces away, the runner is safe at first. If the ball hits the baseline glove and stops within one foot of it, the hitter is awarded second base.

- The fielder must wait until the ball passes the glove before she makes a play.

- Hitters reach base safely on these occasions: (1) Defense makes errors; (2) Defense fields the ball in front of the glove; (3) Hitters beat out the bunt. Runners advance only one base at a time. They cannot advance on wild pitches, steals, or hit batsmen.

- Hitters can drag bunt. They cannot fake bunt and swing away or attempt a squeeze bunt.
- If all three batters load the bases, they must clear the bases and start again. No penalty.
- After three outs, Team A goes on defense; Team B comes to bat. Time dictates the number of innings played.

Twelve Up

Objective: To practice offensive and defensive skills.

Procedure: Two teams, six players per team, bring rubber bases, gloves, bats, and balls to an open area. They make a diamond, bases approximately 50 feet apart.

Play begins when Team A, defense, takes the field. The catcher wears full protective gear; e.g., chest protector, face mask, and shin guards.

Team B, offense, sends a player to first base. A batter comes to the plate. *Objective:* To score runs; it's the hitter's job to advance the runner.

The batter receives two pitches per time at bat. She must bunt one of the pitches. Every player bats twice each inning. If the batter fails to bunt the ball into fair territory, she's out; she returns to the end of the line.

The pitcher throws to 12 batters each inning. If the pitcher fails to throw strikes or hits the batter, the batter takes first base. The next girl in line comes to the plate.

After three outs, runners leave the base and return to the end of the line. After every hitter bats twice, sides change regardless of number of outs. Team B takes the field; Team A comes to bat.

Runners advance on walks, wild pitches, passed balls, errors, bunts, or steals (if they are part of offensive strategy). Runners leave the bases after three outs. Another player goes to first base and play continues. Caution runners not to slide or interfere with play.

The team scoring the most runs in six innings wins. Extra laps or push-ups for the losing players adds zest to the game.

The coach makes defensive and offensive changes. The offensive team, by prearranged signals, can execute several plays—suicide or safety squeeze, run and bunt, fake bunt and run, and so on. Fielders can work on base coverage, making force-outs, trapping players in rundowns, stopping the squeeze, etc.

Make sure all players stay busy and that athletes play their normal positions. Extra players can work individual or small group drills until the coach calls for them.

BUNTING FOR THE BASE HIT

Some athletes think that it takes great speed to bunt for the base hit. Admittedly, a player fast afoot has an advantage, but an athlete with average speed can do an admirable job. Two ingredients—concentration and bat control—largely determine bunting success.

An athlete adept at handling the bat may occasionally use the push-bunt technique to reach base safely. However, we'll center our attention on the drag-bunt method. Let's begin by examining how a batter (right-handed) can bunt for the base hit.

- Assume a normal stance. Be careful not to tip your hand or cause suspicion. Move close to the front of the box.
- After the pitcher releases the ball, drop right foot back between four to six inches.
- Turn slowly toward the pitcher, bending at the knees and waist.
- Pull left elbow toward waist and slide right hand several inches toward the label of the bat.
- Keep head still. Fix eyes on the ball. Hold the bat parallel to the ground.
- Watch the ball hit the bat. Drop it down the third base line by tipping the fat end of the bat toward third base. Both feet, pointing toward first base, are in excellent position for a quick take-off (Figure 11.4).

A good time to drag bunt is when the third baseman is playing deep, standing flat-footed, or paying attention to something other than the ball game. Also, if the pitcher keeps her deliveries on the outside corner, drop it down.

BASE-HIT BUNTING DRILLS

If your athletes are serious about developing into excellent bunters, offer them these drills to work alone, with a partner, or in a small group:

Figure 11.4

Individual Bunting Drills

Fast Break

Objective: To practice getting a good jump toward first.

Procedure: Go to an open area. Assume normal batting stance. Imagine a pitcher winding up and releasing the ball. Bunt the "pitch" down the third base line and break for the first base. Fire out of the batter's box by driving hard off the right foot. Run about 20 feet and stop. Repeat several times.

Toss-Up Bunt

Objective: To bunt the ball in fair territory and get a good jump to first.

Procedure: Bring a glove, bat, and ball to an open area. Set the glove about 25 feet up the third base line. Assume normal batting stance. Toss a ball into the air, drag bunt it down the third-base line, and break for first base. Try to bunt the ball on or near the glove. Repeat several times.

Partner Bunting Drills

Sprint to First

Objective: To practice getting a fast start to first.

Procedure: Bring a partner, rubber base (first base), and stop watch to an open area. Set the base about 60 feet away. Repeat the procedure for "Fast Break." Now have your partner time you to first base and correct any faults she sees.

Half Way

Objective: To practice bunting the ball and breaking toward first.

Procedure: Place the rubber base about 30 feet away. Have partner stand approximately 40 feet away and throw one-half speed. Bunt the ball down the third base line. Try to reach first before partner fields the ball.

Note: Your partner cannot break for the ball until it hits the ground. Keep the drill competitive by adjusting the base distance until you can reach first a split second before your partner touches the ball.

Small-Group Bunting Drills

Competition Bunt

Objective: To practice bunting with accuracy.

Procedure: Four athletes go to an open area. Player 1 and Player 2 stand about three feet apart near the third-base line. Player 3, pitcher, stays 40 feet away from Player 4, batter.

Player 4 receives three pitches. She attempts to lay down a drag bunt between Player 1 and Player 2. Both players remain still until after the ball stops rolling. Award one point for each successful bunt. After three bunts, athletes rotate clockwise. The athlete with the most points after 15 bunts wins.

Bunt/Double Toss

Objective: To practice bunting the ball and breaking toward first.

Procedure: Four athletes bring three rubber bases to an open area. They set up a diamond, bases about 60 feet apart. Player 1, fielder, stands near third base; Player 2, fielder, stays near first base; Player 3, pitcher, stands 40 feet away from Player 4, batter.

Action begins as the pitcher delivers the ball. Player 4 drag bunts the ball toward Player 1 and sprints to first base. Player 2 breaks for second, receives a throw from Player 1, then makes a relay throw to Player 3, covering first base. Player 1 is the only athlete allowed to field the bunt.

Again, adjustments for playing conditions, player speed, and space availability must be made. Caution fielder not to cheat by charging before the ball hits the ground. Also, remind Player 1 and Player 2 to make chest-high, glove-side throws.

After the batter bunts the ball and runs to first, have players rotate clockwise. Award two points to the batter every time she beats the play; subtract one point when she fails to beat the throw. The first athlete to earn ten points wins.

BUILDING CONFIDENCE IN BUNTING

Athletes who have trouble bunting the ball need to be reassured that they can succeed. As a coach, you must seek ways to help athletes become better bunters. Here are six ways to instill confidence in your players:

1. Stress the importance of bunting. Make sure athletes understand why the bunt is critical at certain times. The best way to convince athletes is to make bunting an important part of practice.

2. Show players how the bunt can work to their advantage; i.e., increase on-base percentage, increase batting average, command respect from the defense, and so forth. Demonstrate, by setting up offensive strategy during practice, how bunting adds an extra dimension to the team's overall scoring punch.

3. Offer words of encouragement. Make athletes aware that bunting is a skill worth developing and it takes time to become proficient.

4. Pass out available printed material on bunting techniques. Make copies to distribute to your athletes.

5. Urge athletes to spend extra time on their own practicing bunting skills. Pass along tips and suggestions for setting up activities

and drills. Relate how competitive partner and small-group drills make practice challenging and fun.

6. Have athletes approach the art of bunting with patience. Tell them to master each skill one step at a time. For example, if an athlete wants to learn to drag bunt, she should work on bunting the ball with the fat end of the bat before breaking toward first.

TIPS AND SUGGESTIONS FOR BETTER BUNTING

Now that your athletes feel confident about their bunting ability, give them these pointers to keep in mind:

1. Stay up front in the batter's box. This makes it easier to bunt the ball in fair territory.
2. Keep eyes fixed on the ball until it makes contact with the bat.
3. Stress bunting the ball down the baseline into fair territory.
4. Keep the bat steady. Never lunge or go after the pitch. "Catch" the ball on the bat.
5. Make sure the ball is bunted on the ground before running to first.
6. Hold the bat parallel to the ground. This reduces the number of fouled or missed pitches.
7. Extend arms, bending them at the elbows. Keep the bat well in front of home plate.
8. When ready to bunt, square around and face the pitcher. Be careful not to give yourself away too soon.
9. Set your mind to bunt a good pitch, one that you can handle with minimum difficulty.
10. Develop patience. Be selective. And bunt the pitch you want.

POINTS TO REMEMBER

When an athlete develops into a proficient bunter, several things occur: one, she sharpens her ability to control the bat; two, she learns how to take advantage of lazy opponents; three, she advances runners into scoring position; and four, she increases her chance of reaching base safely.

Bunting, like any other softball skill, can be perfected if the athlete is willing to work hard at it. An athlete becomes a double threat when she combines both bunting and hitting skills.

You can help an athlete believe in herself by offering positive advice, constructive criticism, and constant encouragement.

12. Hitting

MANY SOFTBALL COACHES agree that hitting is the most difficult skill to teach. An athlete may have the physical ability to be an outstanding hitter, but allows a slump or a pitcher with a reputation for striking out batters to beat her mentally. In short, the coach must seek ways to develop an athlete mentally as well as physically.

In this section we'll discuss these areas:

1. Examining the physical side of hitting
2. Examining the mental side of hitting
3. Individual hitting drills and activities
4. Small-group hitting drills, activities, and games
5. Hitting drills for the entire team
6. Ways to help athletes break the batting slump
7. Tips and suggestions for successful hitting
8. Points to remember

EXAMINING THE PHYSICAL SIDE OF HITTING

No two athletes bat exactly alike. Each athlete develops her own style of hitting and tends to use those techniques which produce the best results. Following is a description of the key points in batting to pass along to your players.

Stance

The batter must be relaxed with her body weight balanced comfortably over her feet. She should be close enough to the plate so her bat can reach pitches nipping the outside corner. She should also be up in the box (near the front edge of home plate) so she can make solid contact with pitches before they curve, rise, or drop.

The stances most hitters use are parallel, open, and closed. An athlete who uses a parallel stance stands with her feet shoulder width apart, parallel to home plate (Figure 12.1).

The open stance (Figure 12.2) shows the hitter placing the lead foot farther away from the inside edge of the plate than the rear foot. This is a good stance to use when facing a fast pitcher because it gives the batter a better look at the ball, it allows her to swing faster, and it shortens the swing.

The closed stance (Figure 12.3) shows the hitter placing the lead foot closer to the inside edge of the plate than the back foot. This stance is used against slower pitchers to keep the hitter from pulling the ball and to hit the pitch to the right side of the field.

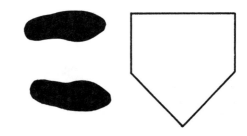

Figure 12.1

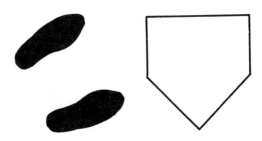

Figure 12.2

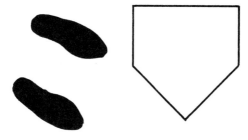

Figure 12.3

Grip

Basically, the grip controls the swing and regulates bat speed. Therefore, a hitter should stress these points:

- Hold the bat at the base of the fingers against the calloused part of top hand.
- Do not hold bat in palm. This restricts the amount of wrist snap.
- Align the knuckles of both hands.
- Use a firm, but relaxed grip. At the beginning of the swing, if someone walked up and grabbed the bat and twisted it, it should turn in the batter's hands.
- Keep a firm grip throughout the swing.

Four Common Grips

1. *Standard*—The batter grips the bat about one or two inches from the knob.
2. *Choke*—The batter holds the bat about four to six inches from the knob. This grip works well against a fast pitcher since the batter has better control of her swing and increases her chances of making solid contact with the pitch.
3. *Long Grip*—The batter holds her hands together next to the knob. She uses this grip when hitting for power and when facing a slow pitcher.
4. *Split Grip*—The batter places her top hand several inches above bottom hand. This grip tends to shorten the length of the swing and helps the hitter gain bat control.

Bat Position

Bat position signals a batter's readiness to hit the ball. At this point the physical and mental forces join together to spring into action. Here are four guidelines to give your athletes:

1. Hold bat in a horizontal position. Point end of bat toward backstop, not up in the air.

2. Hold arms out away from body, flexed at the elbows. Extended arms allow the hitter to pull the bat ahead with bottom hand and roll top hand over to obtain a sharp wristsnap.

3. Hold bat at top of strike zone. Any pitch above this level would not be a strike. The bat swing moves through a slightly downward path.

4. Keep all movement going in a forward direction. Once the swing begins, carry it through completely.

Stride and Swing

Once the batter decides to swing, her stride carries her body into position to hit the ball. The stride and swing must work together to bring the bat around in a smooth manner. Give your athletes the following information:

1. Keep body weight evenly distributed over both feet. Turn hips slightly back toward the catcher.

2. Hold head still, fix eyes on the ball.

3. While waiting for the pitch, shift weight to the rear foot. As the pitcher releases the ball, stride forward with the front foot. This forward motion allows the arms, shoulders, and hips to rotate in unison.

4. Fully extend the arms out in front of home plate. Keep head down and watch the ball hit the bat. Power comes from the arms and wrists.

5. Concentrate on rolling wrists as the bat hits the ball.

6. Bring the bat completely around so the bat ends up at a point beyond the front shoulder.

EXAMINING THE MENTAL SIDE OF HITTING

It has been said that hitting is about 75 percent mental. As a coach, you can show athletes how to build confidence and develop a positive mental approach. Here are seven suggestions to give your athletes:

1. While sitting on the bench, watch the pitcher. Try to pick up a pitching pattern or any sign or mannerism from the pitcher that signals a certain pitch is coming.

2. Think success. Picture yourself in your mind's eye making solid contact with the pitched ball. Rehearse this mental event until it forms a permanent image.

3. Believe in your ability to hit. If you are not successful the first few times, gird yourself to do well the next time you step to the plate.

4. Evaluate your performance. Record your weaknesses and prescribe a plan for improvement. Then set your plan into action by working hard in practice.

5. Be flexible. Adjust to the pitcher's deliveries. As an example, if the hurler throws with exceptional speed, choke up and stress contacting the ball with the fat part of the bat. If the hurler throws many breaking pitches, move up in the batter's box and hit the ball before it breaks.

6. Seek continual improvement. Don't be satisfied with an average performance.

7. Concentrate on the task at hand. Avoid distractions which take your mind off of hitting the ball.

INDIVIDUAL HITTING DRILLS AND ACTIVITIES

Players often ask, "What can I do on my own to become a better hitter?" The answer is simple: *Practice.* The best way to improve hitting skills is to hit. And if your athletes plan to work out alone, provide them with these six activities:

Mirror Swing

Stand in front of a full-length mirror. As you swing the bat, check your technique. Stop and make corrections when you spot a problem. Continue swinging with a complete follow-through for approximately ten to fifteen minutes.

Weighted Bat

Develop strength in the forearms, hands, and wrists by swinging a weighted bat at least ten minutes a day. This is an excellent off-season activity to develop arm and shoulder muscles in preparation for the coming season.

Target Zone

Make a strike zone target out of cardboard or plywood (Figure 12.4). Paint a square in each corner about the size of a softball. Hang the target on a bush, fence, tree, or garage door. Make sure the corner squares match the knee/shoulder level of the strike zone. Stand about ten feet away and face the target. Practice swinging at each of the four corners.

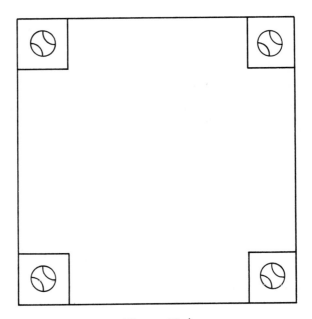

Figure 12.4

Imaginary Pitch

Assume normal batting stance. Visualize a pitcher winding up and releasing the ball. Say to yourself, "Left Field" or "Center Field" or "Right Field." Swing in the called direction. Picture in your mind's eye meeting the ball squarely in front of home plate. "See" the ball landing safely in fair territory.

Off the Tee

Obtain a batting tee. Set it up so that you hit balls into a net or backstop. Concentrate on extending the arms and hitting the ball with the fat end of the bat. Try to hit balls straight up the middle.

Fungo Up

Stand in front of a net, sideline fence, or backstop. Toss a ball into the air and hit it straight ahead. Again, stress making contact with the fat end of the bat. Keep eyes on ball, extend arms, and fungo low line drives.

SMALL GROUP HITTING DRILLS, ACTIVITIES, AND GAMES

Two advantages of holding small-group hitting drills are: One, athletes stay busy moving at a rapid pace; Two, several small groups can work simultaneously in different areas of the field.

Let's begin by examining four-man hitting drills.

Go the Other Way

Objective: The batter practices hitting the pitched ball into the opposite field.

Procedure: Four players—pitcher, batter, and two fielders —go to an open area, preferably near a fence. Place a rubber base (home plate) near the fence. The pitcher stands approximately 40 feet away from home plate. The two fielders remain about 150 feet away from home plate.

Action starts when a batter comes to home plate. If she's a right-hander, both fielders move to left field. Conversely, if she bats from the left side, both fielders move to right field. The pitcher, throwing one-half to three-quarters speed, concentrates on hitting the outside corner of home plate. Tell the pitcher to throw only straight pitches and stress control.

When the pitcher releases the ball, a fielder races toward the opposite field. The batter tries to drive the ball in front of the moving fielder. Fielders trade off running down the ball. The fielder, waiting her turn, retrieves balls hit into the wrong field or behind the sprinting fielder.

The streaking fielder gives the batter an excellent target analogous to a quarterback leading a receiver. A hitter, using a choke grip with an easy swing, should do well. She will realize the importance of watching the pitched ball carefully. The pitcher controls the pace of action. She must concentrate on keeping the ball on the outside corner of home plate.

Behind Second

Objective: To stress hitting the ball up the middle of the diamond.

Procedure: Four players—pitcher, batter, infielder, and outfielder—go to an open area, preferably near a fence. Use rubber bases for second base and home plate. The pitcher stands approximately 60 feet away from home plate. The baseman stays about 20 feet behind second base. The outfielder remains 30 to 50 feet directly behind the infielder.

Action begins when a batter comes to home plate. The pitcher, throwing one-half to three-quarters speed, concentrates on tossing strikes. The batter receives six swings.

She attempts to hit the ball somewhere between the baseman and outfielder. Award points as follows:

1 point —Any hard hit ball; i.e., line drive or grounder.

2 points—Any ball which drops between the infielder and out-fielders (excluding pop flies). If a fielder bobbles the ball, the batter receives an extra point.

0 points—Pop flies which land between fielders.

Each hitter goes around twice. Players rotate clockwise; i.e., hitter plays the outfield, outfielder moves behind second base, infielder becomes pitcher, and pitcher becomes hitter. The athlete earning the most points wins.

A softball glove placed 20 to 30 feet to the left and to the right of the outfielder marks a target zone for the hitter. Fielders judge whether or not balls land within the target area. Each batter should stress these skills:

- Watch the ball carefully.
- Use an easy swing with a complete follow-through.
- Use a slight choke for better bat control.
- Meet the ball squarely in front of home plate.
- Hit with a still head.

Punch and Bunt

Objective: To practice place-hitting and bunting the pitched ball.

Procedure: Four players—pitcher, batter, and two fielders
—go to an open area, preferably near a fence.
Use rubber bases for first base, third base, and
home plate. The pitcher stands about 40 feet
away from home plate. One fielder takes third
base; the remaining fielder plays first base.

Action begins when a batter comes to home plate. The pitcher
throws one-half to three-quarters speed. The batter receives five
chances to hit the ball. She follows this pattern:

First Swing   —Hits ball to third baseman.

Second Swing—Hits ball to first baseman.

Third Swing   —Hits ball back to the pitcher.

Fourth Swing —Bunts ball to the third baseman.

Fifth Swing   —Bunts ball to the first baseman.

Award points in the following manner:

1 point   —For every ball hit or bunted fair to the designated
player.

½ point   —For every ball hit or bunted fair regardless of
where it goes.

3 point bonus —For hitters who satisfactorily complete the cycle; i.e., hit or bunt all five pitches to the correct players.

Lose all points—Any hitter who misses or fouls a bunt attempt.
She must begin a new point total.

Each batter goes around three times. Athletes rotate clockwise;
i.e., hitter goes to third, third baseman moves to first, first baseman
takes the mound, and pitcher becomes hitter. The first player earning
fifteen points wins.

The drill's success hinges on the pitcher's ability to throw
strikes. Batters should stress swinging at strikes only. They should go
with the pitch; that is, hit outside pitches to the opposite field, pull
inside pitches, and drive pitches down the center of home plate up
the middle of the diamond.

Now let's look at a popular five-man drill:

Liner Through

Objective: To concentrate on hitting the ball up the middle of the diamond.

Procedure: Two five-man teams compete. Team A, offense, comes to bat. Team B, defense, takes the field. Team B athletes position themselves in the following manner.

- Player 1—Pitcher, throws one-half to three-quarters speed.
- Player 2—Catcher, wears full protective gear.
- Player 3—Left field, medium deep.
- Player 4—Center field, medium deep.
- Player 5—Right field, medium deep.

Here are the rules for "Liner Through":

- Each hitter receives one swing per time at bat. A called strike, missed swing, or foul ball counts as a time at bat. The catcher acts as judge.
- Each player on the team comes to bat three times before taking the field.
- Only hypothetical runners are used. Runners advance on base hits only. They cannot advance on passed balls, wild pitches, errors, or hit batsman. Runners move one base at a time. *Exception:* A double advances a runner two bases.
- The batter has one objective: to hit the ball up the middle of the diamond into center field. All balls hit up the middle between the pitcher and center fielder count as doubles. All other pitches hit into fair territory (ruled by the catcher as base hits) go as singles. A double is the longest hit a player can get.
- A player makes an out if she swings and misses, pops up to a fielder, fouls the pitch, hits a ground ball, line drive, or fly ball into the outfield (unless otherwise ruled a base hit). A player is out if she hits a ball over an outfielder's head.
- Each team comes to bat four times (optional). Every player receives 12 swings.

Comment: Athletes try for base hits, not long home runs. "Liner Through" requires each hitter to use a smooth, easy swing for positive results. This is an excellent activity to use at the end of practice.

Here are two fast-moving six-man drills:

Fungo Away

Objective: To practice hitting (fungoing) and scoring runs.

Procedure: Six players carry rubber bases, gloves, bats, and balls to an open area in the field. Athletes make a diamond, bases approximately 60 feet apart. Athletes position themselves in the following manner:

Player 1—First hitter

Player 2—Second hitter

Player 3—Catcher

Player 4—Left field, medium deep

Player 5—Center field, medium deep

Player 6—Right field, medium deep

Here are the rules:

- Player 1 comes to home plate, tosses a ball into the air, and hits it somewhere into the outfield. She runs the bases, going as far as possible.
- The outfielders, working together, attempt to put out the runner. For example, if the batter hits a ball into center field, the left fielder covers second or third hoping to tag the runner out. Outfielders decide how they want the bases covered.
- The second hitter, Player 2, must score her partner. If she fails, her partner is out and returns to home plate. Player 1 becomes the hitter.
- After three outs, athletes rotate. Player 1 becomes Player 2, Player 2 becomes Player 3, and so on.
- Athletes make outs when they: 1. Fly out, pop out, or line out to a fielder, including the catcher; 2. Miss or foul the ball; 3. Interfere with play, run out of the base line, etc.; 4. Fail to touch a base; 5. Hit the ball into the infield; 6. Hit the ball over an outfielder's head; 7. Attempt to steal or slide; 8. Leave the base before the batter hits the ball.
- Each player keeps track of runs scored. The player scoring the most runs wins.

On the Target

Objective: To practice hitting and fielding.

Procedure: Six players carry rubber bases, six old towels, gloves, bats, and balls to an open area in the field near an outfield or sideline fence. Athletes make a diamond, bases approximately 60 feet apart. Players position themselves in the following manner:

Player 1—Hitter

Player 2—Pitcher, throws one-half speed.

Player 3—Rover, plays anywhere between the pitcher and outfield. The hitter can move the rover to any spot on the field.

Player 4—Left field, medium deep.

Player 5—Center field, medium deep.

Player 6—Right field, medium deep.

Two towels are placed 15 to 20 feet apart in a horizontal position with home plate marking the target zone. A target area appears in left field, center field, and in right field.

Action begins when Player 1 comes to home plate. She receives six swings. Her object is to hit the pitched ball into the target areas. Hitters earn extra points as follows:

3 points—Ball hits the target area; i.e., lands on or between the towels. Outfielder acts as judge. She cannot field the ball before it hits the ground unless it carries beyond the target area.

2 points—Ball lands near the target zone (within three or four feet)

1 point —Fielders bobble the ball or play it before it reaches the target area. *Exception:* Ground balls hit into the outfield.

0 points—Balls landing outside the target area.

After six swings the players rotate to the next number; i.e., Player 1 becomes Player 2, Player 2 becomes Player 3, and so forth. The athlete earning the most points after two rounds wins. Comments: Hitters try to punch the ball over the rover's head into the target zone. If a player (right-hander) wishes to hit inside pitches into left field, she tells the pitcher to keep balls on the inside corner of home plate. She may also wave the rover toward the third base line. A player usually succeeds if she uses a choke grip, watches the ball closely, swings easily, and hits the ball where it is pitched.

HITTING DRILLS FOR THE ENTIRE TEAM

Keeping every one busy during batting practice is a tall order. The following four activities give each athlete something to do:

Choke-Grip Punch

Objective: To make contact with the pitched ball.

Procedure: Divide team into four or five groups, four players per group. Send each group to a different part of the field, preferably near a fence.

Player 1, batter, stands near the fence. Player 2, pitcher, stays approximately 40 feet away facing Player 1. Players 3 and 4, fielders, remain close together behind the pitcher. Player 3 stands to the right of Player 2; Player 4 keeps to the left of Player 2.

Action begins when Player 2 pitches the ball to Player 1. Player 3 breaks to her right; Player 4 runs about 40 feet to her left. The batter, using a choke grip, punches the ball toward Player 3. Player 3 fields and throws the ball to Player 4. Player 4 returns the ball to Player 2.

Player 1 receives two pitches. She hits the first delivery to Player 3, the second to Player 4. Athletes rotate clockwise. Award points as follows:

2 points—The fielder makes a clean play, including a good throw.

1 point —The batter hits the ball to the correct fielder.

0 points—A batter receives no points if she does the following: Hits a ball the fielder cannot reach; hits a pitch to the wrong fielder; or misses or fouls the pitch. A fielder receives no points if she bobbles or throws the ball wildly. The first player earning ten points wins.

Situation

Objective: To practice hitting and allow athletes to work on fielding, running, and throwing skills.

Procedure: Go to the baseball diamond. Select two full teams, nine players per team.

Action begins when Team A, defense, takes the field. The catcher wears full protective equipment. Team B, offense, sends a player to first base. A batter comes to the plate. She receives three pitches; each pitch presents a different situation. They are as follows:

Situation One, first pitch—The batter has a 3-1 count; she must execute a hit-and-run on the *first* pitch.

Situation Two, second pitch—The hitter must bunt the *second* pitch.

Situation Three, third pitch—The hitter can bunt or swing away on the *third* pitch. Hitters run out the last swing.

A batter makes an out if she swings and misses on any pitch, fouls the pitch, or takes a called strike. She reaches base on walks (pitcher misses on all three deliveries), catcher's interference, errors, being hit by the pitch, or base hits. The batter runs out the third pitch only; runners, however, go every time the batter hits the ball. Runners advance on base hits, errors, wild pitches, tag-ups, or passed balls. No stealing is allowed (Exception: hit-and-run).

Every player bats twice each inning. The pitcher throws to 18 batters. After three outs, runners leave the bases and return to the end of the line. Another player goes to first base and play continues. After every hitter bats twice, sides change regardless of number of outs. Team B takes the field; Team A comes to bat. The catcher (designated player or coach) umpires the game. Caution pitchers to throw half-speed. Warn runners not to slide or interfere with play. The team scoring the most runs wins.

Bring Her Around

Objective: Same as "Situation."

Procedure: The same as "Situation" with the following additions:

- Team A, offense, sends a batter to the plate. Two players become base coaches.
- The offensive team must follow these rules:

1. The batter must use a choke grip with a smooth, easy swing and follow-through.

2. Players rotate clockwise; e.g., hitter becomes third base coach, third base coach becomes first base coach, first base coach moves to the end of the line, and so on.

3. Athletes only rotate when the batter makes an out; for example, grounds out, fouls out, or strikes out.

4. When runners reach first, first and second, or first and third, the batter must bunt the ball. If bases are loaded, or runners on second and third, or second or third only, the batter swings away. The batter runs everything out.

5. The batter receives two pitches, but only one swing. If she takes a strike, she is out. If the hurler misses on both deliveries, the batter walks.

Comments: The batter realizes she has one chance to make contact with the ball. She knows she must watch the ball every second and not develop the bad habit of taking close pitches. This drill forces the batter to concentrate. A player who swings at one particular pitch seldom experiences success.

Six-Station Circuit

Objective: To practice various hitting skills.

Procedure: Break team into small groups, two athletes per group. Set up a batting circuit around the playing field (Figure 12.5). Each group works for five minutes at a designated station before moving on. One coach can keep time and supervise the hitting area while another coach works with the remaining players.

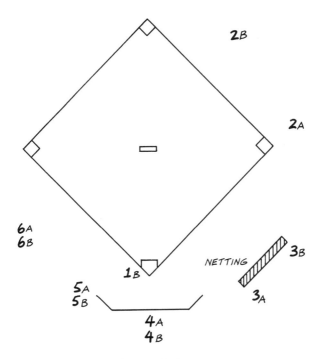

Figure 12.5

Your coaching situation—number of coaches, number of players, available facilities, etc.—will determine the number of activities in the circuit and how many athletes in each group. If you want to set up a six-station circuit, here are the activities you might wish to include:

Player	What Does Player Do?
1A	Feeds the pitching machine
1B	Hits the ball
2A	Hits off the tee
2B	Fields the batted ball
3A	Hits tossed ball into netting (Player 3B stands to side and lobs ball to Player 3A)
3B	Lobs ball to Player 3A
4A	Bunts the ball
4B	Pitches the ball
5A	Swings weighted bat (full cut with follow-through)
5B	Swings weighted bat (practices rolling the wrists)
6A	Swings ball attached to a rope (see note)
6B	Hits the ball

Note: Drill a hole through the center of a regulation softball. Thread a rope through the hole being sure to tie a knot on each side of the ball. Then Player 6A stands to the side of Player 6B and swings the rope around her at about waist level. Player 6B attempts to hit the ball as it comes around. Player A can make the ball rise and drop by swinging the rope at different angles.

**WAYS TO HELP ATHLETES
BREAK THE BATTING SLUMP**

The batting slump plagues every softball player at some time in her career and it occurs when the batter fails to make solid contact with the pitched ball. Hitting problems vary. The batter may blink at the last second causing her to miss the pitch or a slight head jerk might throw her timing way off.

Following are eight common batting faults with activities designed to help eliminate them.

Overstriding

A batter who swings too hard may develop this bad habit. She feels a long stride and fast swing are necessary to drive the ball a long distance into the outfield. However, a smart pitcher will change the speed of her pitches to keep the hitter off-balance. Frequently a long stride develops a hitch in the batter's swing. Some hitters stride before they know where the pitch is going. They stay off-balance and fail to make solid contact with the ball. As the pitcher releases the ball, the hitter (right-hander) moves her hands past her right shoulder, drops the end of the bat, and swings in an upward direction.

Activity One

A pitcher, catcher, hitter, three fielders, and the coach participate. The pitcher throws at three-quarter speed. The batter hits six or seven pitches using her normal swing and stride. Then the hitter shortens her stride about four or five inches. A short step (check step) allows the player to reduce her swing and concentrate on the pitched ball. The pitcher mixes her pitches combining fast balls with off-speed deliveries. The coach, standing behind the backstop, can offer helpful suggestions.

Pulling the Lead Foot

Pulling the lead foot or stepping in the bucket carries a batter's head and bat away from home plate. A moving head prevents the hitter from seeing the ball clearly. The pitcher experiences success if she directs her pitches to the outside corner of home plate.

Activity Two

Repeat the procedure for "Activity One." The hitter should emphasize stepping with her lead foot toward the pitcher. This movement keeps the batter's body in a direct line with the pitcher's mound. If the player encounters difficulty, suggest she place a mark, such as scratching an X in the dirt, or laying a piece of cardboard or cloth slightly ahead of her lead foot. Her foot should touch the mark each time she strides toward the pitcher. If the hitter concentrates on driving the ball back through the middle of the diamond, she will keep her eye on the ball and follow through with a smooth, well-coordinated swing.

Tight Grip

An alert catcher knows when a hitter grips the bat too tightly. She watches for the telltale signs such as an incomplete follow-through, locked wrists, or white knuckles.

An athlete locks her wrists when her batting grip prevents the bat from meeting the ball squarely in front of home plate. She either swings down and tops the ball or swings late and fouls the pitch away. Generally, she hits pitches thrown to the inside corner of home plate weakly onto the infield. A comfortable firm grip allows the player to bring the bat around sharply with the wrists, hips, and shoulders rotating in unison.

Activity Three

Repeat the procedure for "Activity One." Have the batter adjust her grip by lining the middle knuckles of her left hand with the middle knuckles of her right hand. This frees her wrists and adds power to the hitter's swing. She will hit inside pitches with greater consistency and make solid contact with the ball.

Let the athlete try different grips. Have her move her hands around until she finds one that feels good. Some batters prefer to rest the middle knuckles of their right hand between the middle and large knuckles of the left hand (right-hander).

Dropping the Far Shoulder

Some batters believe they generate more power by dropping their far shoulder, the shoulder pointing away from the pitcher. They feel a strong, upward swing lifts the ball a long distance into the air. Conversely, uppercutting the ball sends high, pop flies into the infield.

Activity Four

Repeat the procedure for "Activity One." The pitcher stresses throwing high pitches over the inside corner of home plate level with the armpit region of the hitter. The batter soon realizes that she must adjust her swing. If the player lowers her near shoulder, she will automatically lift her far shoulder and bring the bat up higher. Now she swings the bat down on the ball with a greater driving force. A hitter may think she is chopping at the ball, but this downward motion follows a level path. A batter can improve her swing by concentrating on meeting the ball in front of home plate.

Pulling the Outside Pitch

A hitter who tries to pull every pitch makes the pitcher's job easier. The outside corner becomes the hitter's nemesis. For example, a right-handed pull-hitter comes to the plate with no outs, runner at first. The catcher moves her glove to the outside corner of home plate. If the pitcher strikes the catcher's target, the batter will likely hit the ball to the left side of the diamond. The third baseman or shortstop will be busy turning ground balls into force-outs or double plays.

Activity Five

Repeat the procedure for "Activity One." The pitcher keeps the ball on the outside corner of home plate. The fielders shift toward right field. Tell the batter to go with the pitch and hit the ball where it is pitched. A hitter cannot come to the plate assuming she will drive every ball into right field. It is a rare right-handed hitter who can send inside pitches into right field repeatedly. A successful hitter seldom tries to overpower the ball; she concentrates on watching the ball and driving it through the defense.

Poor Bat Control

A wise athlete selects her bat carefully. She finds one that is well-balanced and comfortable to swing. She does not try to wheel the heaviest bat on the rack. A player who swings late, strikes out often, fouls repeatedly or drops the end of the bat may need to change bats. The right bat does not guarantee base hits. A stubborn player may refuse to choke the bat; that is, move her hands up the handle. A batter who insists on gripping the bat near the knob regardless of the situation becomes easy prey for the pitcher. Inside pitches handcuff the batter causing her to hit the ball weakly to third base.

Activity Six

Repeat the procedure for "Activity One." Encourage the hitter to adjust her grip, choke slightly, and swing the bat with a short stroke. She will cut down on her swing and strike out less frequently.

Fault-correcting activities should last approximately 20 minutes and include no more than six athletes. Give each player five minutes of hitting. The pitcher and catcher should coordinate strategy. The pitcher works on control; the catcher studies individual hitting flaws and moves her target accordingly.

Learning the Strike Zone

Some athletes have only a vague idea where the strike zone is. For these players, if a pitch looks good, they simply swing and hope they hit the ball somewhere. Before these athletes can help their team win softball games, they must learn the strike zone. The question is: How? Try this: Have a pitcher, catcher, and batter take the field. If the diamond is occupied, use the areas adjacent to the base lines. A movable rubber base makes a suitable home plate.

The hitter brings a bat to home plate. She doesn't swing the bat. She has three responsibilities: (1) She watches the ball all the way into the catcher's glove; (2) she calls the pitch after it strikes the catcher's glove (ball or strike); (3) she tells the catcher where she *would* hit the ball; i.e., right field, left field, or center field.

Psychologically speaking, a bat in hand gives a player a secure feeling. Although she doesn't swing the bat, she should stride toward every delivery and simulate hitting the ball where it is pitched. The hurler should mix curve balls with fast balls.

Moving Head

When an athlete moves her head, she takes her eyes off the ball. This causes her to miss or foul good pitches. Here's how to get the athlete to keep her head still:

Send batter to home plate. Have a pitcher combine throwing curve balls and fast balls at one-half to three-quarter speed. The batter squares around and bunts the ball toward the mound. She concentrates on bunting the ball with the solid part of the bat.

This activity practically forces the batter to watch the ball hit the bat. The batter soon learns she can make consistent contact with the ball if she keeps her head still.

TIPS AND SUGGESTIONS FOR SUCCESSFUL HITTING

Athletes often become confused and frustrated when they fail to hit the ball hard. Too much advice from too many people tends to overstimulate the nervous system and retard progress. To be sure, teaching an athlete how to hit is a most difficult challenge. A coach needs to be patient and, at the same time, convince the athlete that she can improve if she works hard in practice.

Here are several pointers your athletes may find useful:

1. Meet the ball squarely in front of home plate. Lay the fat part of the ball on the bat.

2. Develop a strong, quick, wristsnap. An athlete can develop strong wrists by swinging a weighted bat.

3. Use a "mean" swing; that is, whip the bat through the ball on contact.

4. Keep body weight forward.

5. Learn the strike zone.

6. Cover the strike zone with your bat. Stand close enough to the plate to ensure complete coverage.

7. Extend arms fully. Drive the bat forward with a powerful thrust.

8. Try to hit the ball when your weight shifts from your right foot to your left foot (right-handed hitter).

9. Keep a still head, fix eyes on the ball, and watch the ball hit the bat.

10. Use a firm, but relaxed grip on the bat.

11. Align fingers of both hands to allow the wrists to break as the bat crosses home plate.

12. Avoid overstriding. A short stride gives you better bat control and reduces head movement.

POINTS TO REMEMBER

Hitting, for most athletes, is a major concern. It seems that supporters ask the same question after a game, "How many hits did you get?" It is a rare athlete who finds satisfaction in saying, "Zero."

Successful hitting requires sound execution of skills and a willingness to spend long hours developing a smooth, natural swing. An athlete must extend a conscientious effort to improve. Once a player refines her hitting skills, she gains self-confidence and increases her value to the team.

The ingredients of a well-coordinated swing include a comfortable stance, firm grip, body weight in balance, full arm-extension, strong wrist-snap, still head, and complete follow-through.

Last point: Encourage athletes to work out on their own every chance they get. Few athletes become razor-sharp in the time allotted in practice.

13. Activities for the Off-Season

ONCE THE SEASON ends, new challenges begin. Questions come to mind such as:

- What were the major weaknesses the team faced this year?
- What were the major strengths?
- What special preparations need to be made before the next year?
- Should athletes participate during the off-season?
- Should athletes be encouraged to play other sports in the off-season?

In this final chapter we'll review these five topics:

1. What should your players do in the off-season?
2. What should you do during the off-season?
3. Conditioning programs and activities.
4. How your athletes can ready themselves for the coming season.
5. Points to remember.

WHAT SHOULD YOUR PLAYERS DO IN THE OFF-SEASON?

The answer, of course, depends upon coaching philosophy and what the athlete herself wants to do. However, a player who comes off a poor year should be encouraged to spend extra time working on her shortcomings.

How, as a coach, can you give direction to an athlete after the season ends? Here is a simple plan to help an athlete improve:

1. After evaluating the athlete's overall performance, list on paper the problem spots.

2. Then suggest ways in which the athlete can eliminate the problem. For example:

Problem Spot	*Suggestions for Remediation*
Throwing; five wild throws in the dirt. Trouble throwing from the right side.	Practice fielding balls hit to the right. Stay low, field, come up throwing. Concentrate on making chest-high throws.

3. Go over the plan with athlete.

4. Make sure the athlete knows where she stands with the team next year, especially if she corrects her faults.

Athletes should stay active after the season ends. They can do this by designing a personal workout plan, playing other school sports, or engaging in recreational activities.

As you know, a coach has limited control over athletes. The best way to influence athletes is to build and maintain a first-rate program. Once the program gains a healthy reputation and athletes know what roles they are expected to play, the program itself acts as the prime motivator to encourage player improvement.

WHAT SHOULD YOU DO DURING THE OFF-SEASON?

This, of course, is an individual matter since no two coaches feel or think exactly alike. Some coaches prefer to stay active and coach other sports; others choose to leave the playing field, take up a hobby or leisure-time activity, and relax.

Try as they may, many coaches cannot escape the smell of baseline chalk dust. Therefore, they spend time in the off-season doing the following:

• Evaluating past-season athletic performance and making necessary adjustments.

• Seeking ways to strengthen the overall program.

- Selecting new personnel or establishing a routine for assistant coaches to follow.
- Inspecting and repairing equipment and facilities.
- Ordering equipment for the upcoming season.
- Preparing pre/postseason conditioning programs for athletes.
- Selling the softball program to school personnel, the community, and to athletes new to the program.

A coach, like a marathon runner, can grow weary from moving too fast. An experienced marathon runner learns how to pace herself so she can finish the race. The coach, too, must plan ahead and face obstacles one at a time.

The key to coaching longevity is renewed enthusiasm. A coach who looks forward to a new season exudes confidence and carries a positive spirit that spreads to athletes. Undoubtedly, the season gets off to a great start.

What can a coach do to renew enthusiasm and prepare mentally for the upcoming season? Here are six things:

1. Browse the library or book store for ''how-to'' books related to coaching techniques. These often provide a fresh outlook on performing strategy, teaching fundamental skills, or planning practice sessions, and so on.

2. Read current articles from coaching magazines that outline innovative drills and activities. Adding one or two new drills in practice from time to time keeps spirits high.

3. Attend softball clinics and workshops. Listen and observe what other coaches and athletes are doing. Exchanging ideas with others provides an excellent learning atmosphere for everyone.

4. Select those drills and activities that athletes favor; then write a magazine article describing these activities, how they were used, and how their use helped the team. Send the article to a coaching magazine. Seeing your article in print may open the door for additional creative ventures.

5. Coach a summer youth team. Teaching youngsters softball skills and watching them develop into outstanding athletes keeps the pilot light burning.

6. Talk softball to anybody who shows the slightest interest. Brag about your program and athletes. Letting others know how you feel, especially if your message carries a positive tone, is a sure-fire way to gain supporters.

CONDITIONING PROGRAMS AND ACTIVITIES

A preseason conditioning program may consist of warm-up and stretching exercises, aerobic conditioning (pitchers and catchers), and aerobic conditioning combined with strength training. Some coaches prepare a booklet of drills and activities for athletes to use prior to the first practice session. These preseason activities may well carry over into the regular season, especially plenty of running for pitchers.

Karen Linde, Sierra College softball coach, runs an off-season conditioning program for her girls that includes a workout three times a week. She expects each athlete to complete the following activities:

1. Stretch hamstrings, quadriceps, calves, back, and shoulder and arm muscles.

2. Squeeze a tennis ball or hand dynamometer 50 times wth each hand.

3. Stand in front of a mirror. Slowly swing a weighted bat. Concentrate on using good form with a smooth wristsnap. Repeat 25 times.

4. Stand in front of a mirror. Take 40 hard swings at an imaginary ball. Again, concentrate on maintaining sound mechanics.

5. Do ten regular full-body push-ups.

6. Make an overhand throw against a wall 30 to 40 feet away. Field the rebound and throw again. Repeat 25 times.

7. Do 25 line-hops. Begin with both feet together on one side of a line. Then hop over the line with both feet and back over the line to the starting position. Do this as fast as possible.

8. Throw a ball as hard as you can into your glove 50 times.

9. Swing a bat at an imaginary pitch and sprint 20 yards as if you were running to first base. Repeat six times.

10. Lead off from a base and do ten takeoffs. Drive strongly for at least five steps.

11. Run one and one-half miles. Alternate running ten 30-yard sprints with ten 50-yard sprints.

Coach Linde includes a short weight-training program at this time. She also arranges individual work for athletes experiencing special problems. Coach Linde holds to a simple philosophy: Structure practice so that everyone knows what to do.

A conditioning program is only as good as the coach's ability to motivate athletes and convince them that hard, consistent practice will maximize player performance. Once an athlete commits herself to excellence, she will contribute greatly to the team's success.

HOW YOUR ATHLETES CAN
READY THEMSELVES FOR THE COMING SEASON

You can help your athletes prepare mentally and physically for the season by holding a preseason team meeting. Here are several tips to stress during the meeting:

Mental Preparation

1. Decide ahead of time what position(s) you wish to try. Study these positions. Know what you are expected to do on defense.

2. Be prepared to play a different position. Do whatever is necessary to help the team win softball games.

3. Set your mind for success. Establish realistic goals, ones that can be reached in a reasonable length of time. Once you make a commitment to achieve these goals, dedicate yourself to carrying out your plans.

4. Seek to constantly improve. Welcome constructive criticism. Discipline yourself to do the best job possible.

5. Keep a positive outlook. Be enthusiastic. Show everyone on the team you came to play.

Physical Preparation

1. Get into shape early in the season. Throw, swing a bat, run wind sprints, and do stretching exercises.

2. Practice hard those skills necessary for playing your desired position(s). For example, an infielder should field plenty of ground balls, an outfielder should shag fly balls, and so on.

3. Execute simple drills and activities on your own, with a partner, or in a small group. Get used to running from side to side, backward, and straight ahead. Practice making chest-high, glove-side throws. Stay low, keep your eyes on the ball, and follow it all the way into your glove.

4. Go 100 percent at all times. Remember, constant hustle shows determination and desire.

POINTS TO REMEMBER

For most coaches, the end of the season brings a sigh of relief. But for some, it signals the beginning of things to come, namely laying plans for next year's team. Returning athletes along with new players provide an incentive for creative thinking.

A team's success depends on several key factors. Athletes must be determined to work hard and do everything possible to help their team win. The coach must offer a well-organized program and allow an athlete the freedom to progress at her own rate.

References

Hoehn, Robert G., *Champ or Chump Drill*, Athletic Journal, Vol. 50, No. 7, March, 1970, p. 30, 100.

Hoehn, Robert G., *Indoor Baseball Games and Drills*, Thomas J. Rowen Booklet Service, 1974.

Hoehn, Robert G., *Baseball Drills for Small Groups*, Thomas J. Rowen Booklet Service, 1975.

Hoehn, Robert G., *Zeroing in on the Shovel/Net Target*, Athletic Journal, Vol. 61, No. 5, January, 1981, p. 34, 76.

Hoehn, Robert G., *Developing Championship Calibre Softball Pitchers*, Coaching Review (The Coaching Association of Canada), Vol. 8, May/June, 1984, pp. 40–42.

Index